£15-95

David Mackay

MODERN ARCHITECTURE IN BARCELONA 1854-1939

BSP PROFESSIONAL BOOKS
OXFORD LONDON EDINBURGH
BOSTON PALO ALTO MELBOURNE

Copyright © Edicions 62, s.a.,
Barcelona 1989

All rights reserved. No part of this
publication may be reproduced, stored
in a retrieval system, or transmitted,
in any form or by any means, electronic,
mechanical, photocopying, recording
or otherwise without the prior
permission of the copyright owner.

This edition first published in Great Britain
by BSP Professional Books 1989

English text first published by
The Anglo-Catalan Society 1985

British Library
Cataloguing in Publication Data
Mackay, David
 Modern architecture in Barcelona (1854-1939)
 1. Spain. Barcelona. Architecture, 1854-1939
 I. Title
 720'.946

ISBN 0 - 632 - 02419 - 4

BSP Professional Books
A division of Blackwell Scientific
Publications Ltd
Editorial Offices:
Osney Mead, Oxford OX2 0EL
(Orders: Tel. 0865 240201)
8 John Street, London WC1N 2ES
23 Ainslie Place, Edinburgh EH3 6AJ
3 Cambridge Center, Suite 208, Cambridge
 MA 02142, USA
107 Barry Street, Carlton, Victoria 3053
 Australia

Set by Anglofort, s.a., Barcelona
Printed in Spain by Grafos, s.a.,
Barcelona, and bound by
Enquadernacions 82, Cornellà (Barcelona)

D.L.: B. 8023 - 1989

Cover
Antoni Gaudí, Casa Batlló
Photography by F. Català Roca

CONTENTS

	INTRODUCTION	7
	List of illustrations	10
I.	THE EARLY ROMANTICS: A SEARCH FOR IDENTITY IN THE PAST	13
II.	THE MODERN ROMANTICS: A SEARCH FOR IDENTITY IN THE PRESENT	27
III.	THE IDEAL ROMANTICS: A SEARCH FOR INSTITUTIONAL IDENTITY	73
IV.	THE UTOPIAN MODERNS: A SEARCH FOR IDENTITY IN THE FUTURE	93
	Location of buildings mentioned in the text	115
	Select bibliography	119

For Roser

INTRODUCTION

There are two questions concerning our culture that have to be examined in order to know where we are, and, if we probe a little more deeply, who we are. They are questions about identity and modernity. The first concerns the understanding of place and memory, the second concerns the understanding of now, the now of present and recent times. These issues remain vital ones, despite the vague and shifting semantic values of the two terms, and despite the current mood of concern that the 'internationalization' of economies and styles tends ever to efface cultural distinctiveness in a uniform modernity.

The circumstances of its recent political and cultural history, and its relative smallness, make Barcelona, the capital city of Catalonia, an excellent laboratory for examination both of these primary questions and of the latter concern. Architecture is the ideal medium through which to explore these issues, for it is a 'total' cultural expression, affected not only by the aesthetic articulation of fashions and ideals but also by the close influence of custom and tradition, by geography itself, and by the reality —aspirations and limitations— of economics, politics and social movements. Architecture thus provides a kind of X-ray of the people who build and inhabit it.

Sharply characterized by the interplay between its specifically local, or national, characteristics and its impulses to relate to the contemporary European cultural scene, Catalan architecture of the nineteenth and twentieth centuries constitutes both a casebook for study of buildings in their context and a focal reference of the continuing discourse on identity and modernity.

The chronology of the survey undertaken in these pages is contained by two dates (1854-1939) whose symbolism is of very different orders but whose significance marks off a coherent 'time-slice' of social and architectural history. Industrialization in the middle decades of the nineteenth century produced a rapid increase in the population of Barcelona: an expanding proletariat and a bourgeoisie anxious to exercise and enjoy its influence. Both these aspects of the modernization of Catalan society required space beyond the restricting walls of medieval Barcelona, demolition of which was begun in 1854. The shape of the modern city began to emerge. The Catalan 'Renaissance', as a fully articulated social and cultural movement, developed apace in an environment which was being adapted quantitatively and qualitatively to its own organic requirements through to the Republican years of the 1930's. 1939 marked a violently abrupt interruption of these processes, by the reactionary forces of a false tradition, but it must be emphasized that this was an interruption and not a termination. All the political and cultural developments in Spain through the last decades of the Franco regime and more dramatically since 1975, not least the undiminished claims of Catalan differentiation, with its linguistic, cultural and institutional manifestations, have made this abundantly clear. Nevertheless a divide can be drawn at 1939, establishing a distance which enables us to view events up to that date with a degree of historical objectivity. A different perspective will be required when the history of the post-war period and its continuities comes to be written.

The four chapters of this book follow for convenience the orthodox classification of modern Catalan culture: the *Renaixença* of the nineteenth century, *Modernisme* bridging the two centuries, the *Noucentisme* of the dawning new century, the Rationalism of the Republican era. There is, though, a unifying line which runs through these phases back to origins in the Romantic movement which defined both the cultural value attached to the artistic product and the notions of national identity associated with history and language. Identifying this thread of Romanticism allows us to see the continuity in the growth of the Modern Movement in architecture and the consolidation of modern culture penetrating the whole complex structure of Catalan society. An understanding of this continuity shows up the artificiality of the conventional labelling and 'freezing' of cultural developments in closed compartments. Thus even the agitated and richly productive central phase, which we designate as *Modernisme*, loses definition as a single, distinctive period or movement when, within this wide vision, we consider the Neo-classical and Romantic legacy absorbed from the preceding *Renaixença* and then the subsequent gradual merging with the Mediterranean classicism of *Noucentisme*. There are, however, no doubts about the singular character of the architecture that was produced in this fertile juncture, responsive to the throb of progress and sharpened to the contrasts of serenity and wildness of the Mediterranean setting.

In Catalonia the dialectics of modernity and individuality establish a particular relationship with international currents and, something by which we are constantly struck, a reluctance to adopt slavishly an anonymous International Style. Munich, Paris and Vienna are present but transformed. This is because the situation and the merchant enterprise of Barcelona make it a city open to trends from all quarters. The city stands at a crossing of cultural trade-routes, more disposed to incorporate and transform its imports than to initiate exportable movements on its own. A focal point of progressive values, but at the same time an institutional capital with natural conservative concerns, the total aspect of Barcelona, an image of Catalan culture as a whole, displays the urge to affirm its cosmopolitanism and a uniqueness of which a certain 'provincialism' is an essential ingredient.

The Catalan case provides an outstanding paradigm to illustrate Christopher Wren's perception that 'Architecture has its political use; public buildings being the ornament of a country; it establishes a Nation; draws people and commerce; makes people love their native country'. With this in mind, and aware that cities are the depositories of our cultural and social inheritance, this casebook of modern architecture is given a framework of reference to major socio-economic and political developments, especially in relation to the gathering momentum of Catalanism. Politics and architecture, as Wren advised, are thus set side by side, the one illuminating the other in a way that it is hoped will make clarification of the past a contribution to the continuing debates of the present.

Some definition of terms is necessary at this stage. *Modern*, according to the Oxford Dictionary, denotes comparatively 'of or pertaining to the present and recent times, as distinguished from the remote past', and, as explained above, the focus here is upon the recent from the standpoint of the present. In the field of art history we observe too that the term *modern* carries a further connotation of 'new-fashioned, not antiquated or absolute'. Now, 'new-fashioned' is ambiguous, because fashion can be and often is regressive, within shifting patterns of taste and market response. We shall consider diverse cases of tension between progress and tradition (or nostalgia) within the Catalan context.

The terms *Modern Movement* or *Modern Architecture* offer no ambiguity or difficulty of interpretation as an international phenomenon. Already in the eighteenth century there was abroad, certainly among intellectuals, what can be considered as a sensibility of change, a sense of belonging specifically to times that were beginning to be so notably different from the past. With the results of industrialization and the political consequences of the French Revolution, awareness of this qualitative difference increased enormously during the nineteenth century. Associated with it were the specific changes that took place, particularly affecting architecture, in the shift of patronage from power and means based on land ownership to the power of production, individual and collective, centred in the towns. Architecture and building, with the time-lag inherent in their rhythms of production, could not but reflect such changes and tensions in the structure of society. Modifications in building typology, technology and new means of production, together with the search for new forms appropriate to new modes of living, all led to a revival of pan-historical styles, and, in an attempt to humanize the machine, to a revival of crafts through which the creative intellectual expressed his engagement in the socialization of culture. The Modern Movement thus implicitly invokes a commitment to progress, from its very origins when that concept acquired ideological force and value.

The term *Modernisme*, on the other hand, refers to a specifically Catalan phenomenon, considered as that stage of the universal Modern Movement which combined the eclectic choice of historical references with the introduction of modern materials, and infused decoration, even construction, with the flowing lines borrowed from the primary source of Nature. It was much more than a local variant of *Art Nouveau* because it became a style identified with a total movement to affirm Catalan nationhood and cultural autonomy, differentiated from Spanishness and attuned to its advanced European counterparts.

This case study of Catalan architecture, focussed centrally but not exclusively on Barcelona, proposes that the resources within the Modern Movement are rich enough to respond to a community's concern with its own identity and modernity, without having to evade the challenge by resorting to sterile historical reproductions. With Cerdà's plan for the expansion of Barcelona, we discover how form can be given to a democratic city structure capable of absorbing the worst of stylistic and speculative assaults. *Modernisme* demonstrates the scope of creative freedom within the discipline of the Cerdà Plan, exploiting a transitional vocabulary set between historicism and the search for unequivocal originality. Under *Noucentisme*, with its preeminent values of the civic image —*la Ciutat*, always with a capital letter, as a physical environment and as a vision of a new Athens— the basis for a public architecture is established. Rationalism enthusiastically embraced the avant-garde, but managed to fit in into the Cerdà framework, either responding to the lyricism of the street or using the buildings to create new urban *milieux*. It is highly significant that the rationalists' buildings were not conceived as isolated art objects but as intrinsic parts of the city as they found it. Their Utopianism harks back ultimately to the *Noucentistes'* ideal City.

The architecture of Barcelona, capital of Catalonia, has had to respond to the politics of place and memory but has always been alive enough to live its history now, with intensity and also with a touch of humour. An understanding of this majestic and exciting city brings with it enriching discoveries about a place, a people and about ourselves as observers of and participants in their culture.

* *

This book was originally published in English in a limited paperback edition by the Anglo-Catalan Society Occasional Publications in 1985. A publication made possible by the untiring efforts of Prof. Alan Yates of Sheffield University. The text did not, and does not, pretend to bring new material to light on the subject of Modern Architecture in Barcelona, but it does try to gather together material from diverse sources to present a more comprehensive picture of Barcelona's contribution to Modern Architecture. Local political and European cultural contexts have been woven into the text to enable us to evaluate just what that contribution has been and to suggest that this Mediterranean capital is not an outsider to European culture.

In this new edition, illustrations have now been added not only as a graphic complement to the text but to trace in its own discipline the dialectics of modernity and individuality which forms part of the essential identity of Barcelona.

D.M.
Barcelona, Autumn 1988.

LIST OF ILLUSTRATIONS

1. Partial view of the gridded city, built following the project of Ildefons Cerdà, 1859.
2. Cerdà, project for the expansion of Barcelona, 1859.
3. Elies Rogent, University of Barcelona, 1868-1872.
4. Joan Martorell, Church of the Salesians, 1882-1885.
5. Antoni Rovira - Josep Fontserè - Josep Cornet, Born Market, 1873-1876.
6. Josep Fontserè, Plant House, 1883-1888.
7. Lluís Domènech i Montaner, Editorial Montaner i Simon, 1880.
8. Josep Fontserè, Reservoir Building, section, 1874-1880.
9. Josep Fontserè, Reservoir Building, ground plan, 1874-1880.
10. Josep Fontserè, Reservoir Building, 1874-1880 (restored in 1988 by Ignacio Paricio, Lluís Clotet and Joan Sabater).
11. Antoni Gaudí, Casa Vicens, 1883-1885.
12. Antoni Gaudí, Casa Vicens, 1883-1885.
13. Josep Vilaseca, Arc de Triomf, 1888.
14. Josep Vilaseca, Casa Pia Batlló, 1891-1896.
15. Josep Vilaseca, Casa Joaquim Cabot, 1901.
16. Lluís Domènech i Montaner, Palau de la Música Catalana, skylight, 1905-1908.
17. Lluís Domènech i Montaner, Palau de la Música Catalana, 1905-1908.
18. Lluís Domènech i Montaner, Cafè-Restaurant, staircase, 1888.
19. Lluís Domènech i Montaner, Cafè-Restaurant, 1888.
20. Lluís Domènech i Montaner, ground floor and main floor plan, 1888.
21. Lluís Domènech i Montaner, Palau de la Música Catalana, detail of the main façade, 1905-1908.
22 - 23. Lluís Domènech i Montaner, Palau de la Música Catalana, ground floor plan and concert hall plan, 1905-1908.
24. Lluís Domènech i Montaner, Palau de la Música Catalana, sculptural group by Pau Gargallo, 1905-1908.
25. Lluís Domènech i Montaner, Palau de la Música Catalana, main façade, 1905-1908.

26 - 27. Lluís Domènech i Montaner, Hospital de Sant Pau, a general view with one of the pavilions, 1902-1910.
28. Lluís Domènech i Montaner, Casa Lleó Morera, 1905.
29. Lluís Domènech i Montaner, Casa Fuster, 1908-1910.
30. Antoni Gaudí, Palau Güell, project of the façade, 1886.
31. Antoni Gaudí, Palau Güell, drawing of the façade as built, 1886.
32. Antoni Gaudí, Palau Güell, 1885-1889.
33. Antoni Gaudí, Casa Calvet, 1899.
34. Antoni Gaudí, Santa Teresa Convent, 1889-1894.
35. Antoni Gaudí, Casa Batlló, 1905-1907.
36. Antoni Gaudí, Casa Milà (La Pedrera - The stone quarry), 1905-1911.
37. Antoni Gaudí and Josep Maria Jujol, Casa Milà, a detail of the ceiling, 1905-1911.
38. Antoni Gaudí, Casa Milà, a detail of the staircase, 1905-1911.
39. Antoni Gaudí, Casa Milà, 1905-1911.
40. Antoni Gaudí, Church of the Sagrada Família, 1884-1926.
41. Antoni Gaudí, Güell Park, 1904-1914.
42. Antoni Gaudí, Bellesguard, 1900-1910.
43. Antoni Gaudí, Bellesguard, 1900-1910.
44. Antoni Gaudí, Güell Gatehouse and Stables, 1887.
45. Antoni Gaudí, Güell Park, 1904-1914.
46. Antoni Gaudí, Church of the Colònia Güell, 1898-1915.
47. Antoni Gaudí, the square in Güell Park, 1904-1914 (drawing by Elies Torres and Martínez Lapeña).
48. Antoni Gaudí, Colònia Güell, plan of the church, 1898-1915.
49. Pablo Picasso, 4 Gats menu, 1899-1900.
50. Josep Puig i Cadafalch, Casa Puig, 1897-1900.
51. Josep Puig i Cadafalch, Casa Quadras, 1904.
52. Josep Puig i Cadafalch, Casa Amatller, 1898-1900.
53. Josep Puig i Cadafalch, Casa Macaya, 1901.
54. Josep Puig i Cadafalch, Casa Macaya, Patio, 1901.
55. Josep Puig i Cadafalch, Casa Terradas (Casa de les Punxes - House of Spires) 1903-1905.
56. Francesc Berenguer, Wine-cellar, Dwellings and Chapel, Garraf, 1888-1890.
57. Francesc Berenguer, Liberty Market, 1893.
58. Josep Puig i Cadafalch, Casarramona Yarn Factory, 1911.
59. Lluís Muncunill, Aymerich i Amat Factory (Terrassa), 1907.
60. Lluís Muncunill, Freixa Farm House converted into factory (Terrassa), 1907.
61. Rafael Masó, Teixidor Flour Mill Factory (Girona), 1910-1911.
62. Josep Pericas, Verdaguer Monument, 1913-1924.
63. Josep Pericas, Church of El Carme, 1910-1914.
64. Josep Goday, Pere Vila School, 1920-1930.
65. Josep Maria Jujol, Torre de la Creu House (Sant Joan Despí), 1913-1916.
66. Josep Maria Jujol, plan of Torre de la Creu House (Sant Joan Despí), 1913-1916.
67. Josep Goday, Baixeras School, 1918-1922.
68. Josep Goday, plan of the Baixeras School, 1918-1922.
69. Josep Maria Jujol, Vistabella Church (Tarragona), 1918-1923.
70. Josep Maria Jujol, plan of Vistabella Church (Tarragona), 1918-1923.
71. Josep Maria Jujol, Vistabella Church (Tarragona), 1918-1923.
72. Josep Maria Jujol, Casa Bofarull (Els Pallaresos), 1914-1931.
73. Josep Maria Jujol, Casa Bofarull (Els Pallaresos), 1914-1931.
74. Josep Maria Jujol, Casa Negre (Sant Joan Despí), 1914-1930.
75. Josep Maria Jujol, Casa Negre (Sant Joan Despí), 1914-1930.
76. Josep Maria Jujol, Casa Planells, 1923-1924.
77. Josep Maria Jujol, plan of Casa Planells, 1923-1924.
78. Francesc Folguera - R. Reventós - M. Utrillo - X. Nogués, Spanish Village, 1927-1929.
79. Ludwig Mies van der Rohe, German Pavilion at the International Exhibition, 1929, rebuilt in 1986.
80. Ludwig Mies van der Rohe, German Pavilion at the International Exhibition, 1929. King Alfonso XIII and Mies van der Rohe at the opening of the Exhibition.
81. Carles Forestier - Carles Buïgas, Illuminated Fountains in Montjuïc, 1929.
82. Francesc Folguera, Casal de Sant Jordi House, 1929-1931.
83. Le Corbusier - GATCPAC, Macià Plan (drawing by Josep Torres Clavé), 1932-1934.
84. Le Corbusier - GATCPAC, Macià Plan (redrawn by X. Monteys), 1932-1934.
85. Francesc Folguera, Casal de Sant Jordi House, 1929-1931.
86. Francesc Folguera, Casal de Sant Jordi House, 1929-1931.
87. Antoni Puig Gairalt, Myrurgia Factory, 1928-1930.
88. Antoni Puig Gairalt, Myrurgia Factory, 1928-1930.
89. Sixt Yllescas, Casa Vilaró, 1929.
90. Ramon Reventós, Apartments in carrer Lleida, 1928.
91. Josep Goday, Collasso i Gil School, 1932.
92. Josep Lluís Sert - Sixt Yllescas, Apartment block in carrer Muntaner, 1930-1931.
93. Joaquim Lloret, Barraquer Clinic, 1936-1939.
94. Joaquim Lloret, Barraquer Clinic, 1936-1939.
95. GATCPAC, Casa Bloc, 1932-1936.
96. Le Corbusier at the Palau de la Generalitat in 1932 during a meeting of the CIRPAC, directive committee of the CIAM.
97. Francesc Folguera, Casa del Llorà (Collsacabra), 1935.
98. Josep Lluís Sert - J. Torres Clavé, Week-end Houses in Garraf, 1935.
99. Josep Lluís Sert - J. Torres Clavé - Joan B. Subirana, Antitubercular Clinic, 1934-1938.
100. Josep Lluís Sert - J. Torres Clavé - Joan B. Subirana, Antitubercular Clinic, 1934-1938.
101 Raimon Duran Reynals, Apartments in carrer Aribau-Camp d'en Vidal, 1934.
102. Josep Lluís Sert - Luis Lacasa, Pavilion of the Republican Government at the Paris Exhibition, 1937.
103. Josep Lluís Sert - Luis Lacasa, Pavilion of the Republican Government at the Paris Exhibition, 1937.

SOURCE OF ILLUSTRATIONS
(The number indicates the illustration)

Arxiu Històric d'Urbanisme, Arquitectura i Disseny, 101. / Arxiu Mas, 36, 50, 53, 54. / Lluís Casals, 75. / Francesc Català Roca, 3, 4, 5, 7, 11, 12, 13, 16, 17, 18, 19, 21, 24, 25, 27, 32, 33, 34, 35, 37, 38, 39, 40, 41, 42, 44, 45, 46, 52, 55, 56, 57, 58, 60, 65, 71, 72, 73, 74, 76, 79, 82, 83, 85, 86, 87, 88, 91, 92, 93, 94, 99, 100, 102, 103. / cb, 22, 23, 30, 31. / Cuadernos de Arquitectura, 98. / Ferran Freixa, 10. / Institut Amatller, 15, 28, 29, 51, 64. / Institut Municipal d'Història, 8, 81. / Lurdes Jansana, 47. / David Mackay, 69. / Duccio Malagamba, 6, 14, 62, 63, 67, 90. / Ricard Marco Muñoz, 2. / Xavier Miserachs, 1, 26. / Museu Picasso, 49. / Poble Espanyol, 78. / Leopoldo Pomés, 43, 59, 61.

Partial view of the gridded city, built following the project of Ildefons Cerdà, 1859.

I
THE EARLY ROMANTICS:
A SEARCH FOR IDENTITY IN THE PAST

From the point of view of the plastic arts, Romanticism was not really a single, coherent code of expression. It was, rather, a new departure away from the prevailing, strict conventions of Neo-classicism and a shift in values which stressed originality in the individual work. In a sense, every building in itself became an occasion. Insofar as there was a recognizable romantic style in architecture, it involved evocation of both classical and medieval cultures, and merged rapidly into an eclectic art that would choose the historical style (or reference) felt to be most appropriate to the work in hand. As Hugh Honour has emphasized, the French Revolution 'sharpened the historical sense in a way that no other event had ever done... To some extent it democratized history by making apparent the influence of political events on ordinary people — and vice versa'. The consequences of this would have inevitable repercussions in architecture.

The eighteenth-century Enlightenment itself, for all its certainties about the natural order of things, generated doubts about the sufficiency of commonly accepted reason. Value came to be placed on the individual and, particularly so in artistic spheres, on the original expression of feeling, elevated to a status competing with that of reason. It became a question of qualities more than of rules, of the soul more than of the brain. With the early Romantics the challenge of shaping a new civilization, almost as a 'tragic' responsibility, is heavy in the air.

The conventional chronological demarcation of European Romanticism —1750-1850— is not really valid for Catalonia. Political, ideological and cultural circumstances in Spain as a whole, over the period in question, account for a distinct time-lag in the assimilation of the values of liberal Romanticism. We can nonetheless detect its appearance in Catalonia from the 1830's and, subsequently, its profound influence on all developments well into our own century.

For convenience, Bonaventura Carles Aribau's *La Pàtria* published in 1833, a nostalgic poem written in 'exile' in Madrid, is persistently cited as the first affirmation of a renewed sense of national identity in Catalonia. Certainly Aribau's sensibility and idiom are distinctly romantic, but the date and the slowness with which the theme was taken up are the clearest evidence of Romanticism's late entry into Catalonia. There are other problems too, associated with the movement's 'nationalist' connotations. The shift in emphasis from a dominant to a 'victimized' sensibility, can be seen to accord with interpretation of the poem as a shimmering dawn of patriotic revival. But Aribau is bidding farewell to the country of his childhood. He dwells on the past and in no way indicates a vision of the present, let alone of the future. This was, in a way, understandable. The extent of the preceding cultural disintegration is not to be underestimated.

Between continuing erosion and newly oppressive Royal Orders, Catalan identity through language, culture and institutions was still receding in the early decades of the nineteenth century. Cultural expression could hardly be a priority for the Catalans in the turbulence of Spanish politics between the War of Independence (1808-1814) and the end of the first Carlist War (1833-1839). During the reign of Isabel I (1840-1868) the Catalan industrial bourgeoisie rose to prominence still supporting the centralized government which provided protectionism, but beginning at the same time to stress their own, and thus Catalonia's, 'differential factor'. However, they also had to deal with social pressures from a growing proletariat, incomprehensible for a Madrid which had yet to feel the full effects of industrialization. These internal tensions were often skilfully diverted away towards the centralist capital, thus tending to create a common cause between capital and labour that was to be channelled into a specifically nationalist discourse. The working class tended to see in the Bourbon monarchy an ulterior force, beyond their immediate employers, that was denying their rights, and was thus drawn into alliance with the Federal Republican movement. This reinforced the sense of Catalan identity, cutting across social classes and creating an unusual condition which provided the fertile ground for popular integration of culture at the end of the nineteenth century.

Catalonia, with its extensive Mediterranean seaboard and its capital in the major port of Barcelona, had prospered historically through its merchant tradition. The industrial revolution took off late here, for reasons alluded to above, but the response was impressive once the appropriate conditions prevailed. The mercantile background enabled local entrepreneurs skilfully to adjust their commercial and home manufacturing tradition to meet the occasion. The historians Josep Termes and Jordi Nadal have pointed out how, on the one hand, the rural

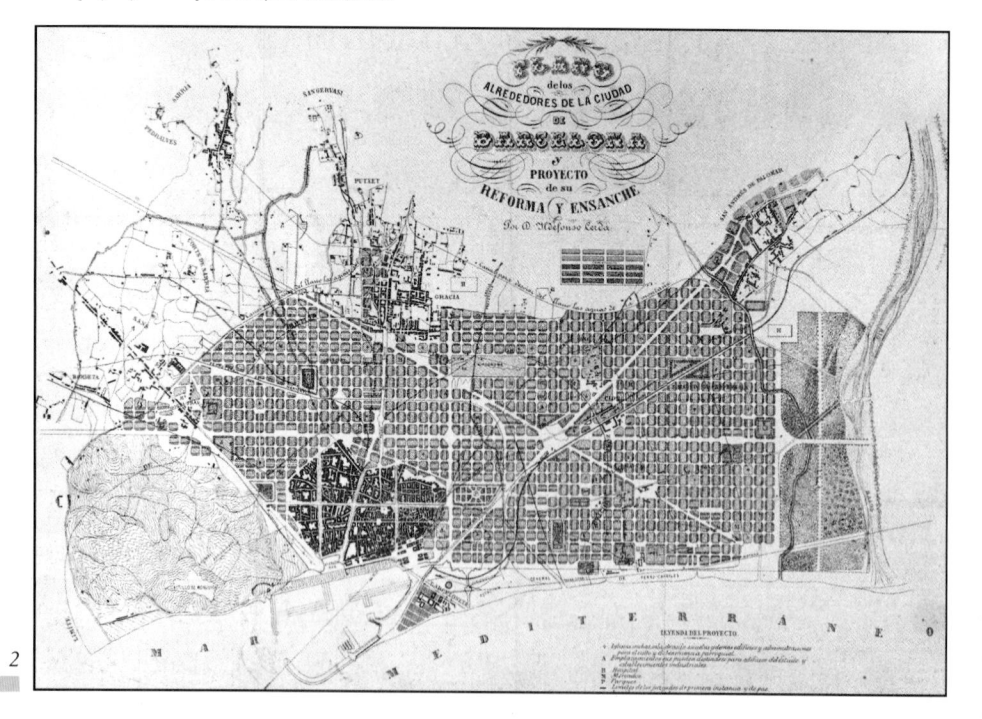

Cerdà project for the expansion of Barcelona, 1859.

population, accustomed to home industry, adapted easily to factory conditions, while, on the other hand, the agile merchant was prepared to take risks (as he always had) in a family industry, assuming the role of capitalist, manager and technician at the same time.

Barcelona's trade with the Americas was reactivated and significantly expanded after 1778, when Seville's official monopoly was finally broken. Cotton was imported from Cuba, where Catalans also settled, and the textile industry flourished along the Ter and Llobregat rivers. With the introduction of the steam engine after 1833 industry expanded vigorously in the cities and along the coast. Besides textiles we find the manufacture of glass, bricks and other ceramics, paper and graphic arts, leather and shoes, chemicals and a small metallurgical industry. However, the basic energy source, coal, had to be imported, and it was only the strict family control over the small factories, together with the inborn knack of a strong merchant tradition, that kept industry buoyant. This industrial advance caused land pressure on Barcelona and other cities, not only for housing the increased urban population but also for its services and institutions. Military and political reasons had prevented the city fathers from increasing the area of Barcelona until popular pressure finally convinced the central government to allow demolition to begin, in 1854, of the walls of the medieval city.

The natural objective was to build on either side of the tree-lined road that linked the small town of Gràcia with Barcelona, across the fields kept clear of buildings within firing range from the old city walls. The immediate need was for a survey map of the area which was produced in 1855 by the Catalan civil engineer Ildefons Cerdà (1815-1876). This first modern topological plan of Barcelona and its surroundings has been the basic instrument of all subsequent development plans for the city, beginning with that produced

Elies Rogent, University of Barcelona, 1868-1872.

by the city architect Miquel Garriga in 1857 which was limited to linking the urban centres of Barcelona and Gràcia. The project contained a grid of 200 m × 140 m with streets 10-20 m wide, and proposed two crescents at either end of a NE-SW axis that were to act as generators to two future radial developments. Apart from being a political exercise to pressurize Madrid into releasing land from military control, the plan probably did not convince the city council. They wanted the sort of results and guarantee that a competition, rather than a single study, would provide. It must be remembered that Baron Haussmann was transforming Paris for Napoleon at that time, and Vienna had also begun to demolish its walls (1857), with a competition for the Vienna Ring being held in 1858.

In 1859 the law was changed to permit the sale of military property, thus allowing the expansion of Barcelona. A competition, based on Cerdà's survey, was arranged by the city authorities and was won by Antoni Rovira (1816-1889). His plan proposed a development in a series of trapezium sectors branching out around the old city, containing lengthening parallel streets 12 m wide, hinged together by wide radial avenues between each sector. The concept was hierarchical, with major and minor spaces and streets, showing the residue of Baroque dominance and display.

Meanwhile Cerdà, after completing his geographical survey, went on to produce a social survey of Barcelona, *Monografía de la clase obrera de Barcelona en 1856*. Here he not only studied groups according to incomes and living expenses but also the dwellings and streets. For example, in housing he found that the rich enjoyed 21 m^2 per person, while craftsmen were limited to 12 m^2 and labourers to 8 m^2, but with the surprising discovery that the latter paid a higher rent for their square metre than the rich for theirs. This direct contact with the reality of urban conditions through his pioneer field-study obviously tempered Cerdà's political attitude. His understanding of these urban conditions, formulated later in the theoretical work *(Teoría general de la urbanización,* 1867), led him to consider communications, density, housing conditions, social and neighbourhood grouping, together with social and other public services of fundamental importance. He was commissioned by the Madrid government to draw up a plan for the reform and extension of Barcelona in February 1859, two months before the city council published the conditions for its own competition. In his plan Cerdà rejected the old hierarchical order of the Baroque city and opted for a more egalitarian and democratic model without class differentiation. In this sense it was a reapplication of neo-classical values. Shocked by the decadence, inhumanity and insanitary conditions of the industrial revolution, but at the same time an engineer committed to science, Cerdà inclined to seek the ideal through reason. An ideal ruthlessly simplified, full of blunt and uncompromising truths. Like Thomas Jefferson, who divided the new territory into a democratic grid of one-mile squares, and like Jean-Nicholas Durand who advocated an economic simplicity in his modular universal building methodology, Cerdà submitted his rational, uniform design for the 'Reform and Extension of Barcelona' to Madrid, where O'Donnell's Liberal Union, subject to pressures for moderation, was in power. It was immediately approved, in spite of Catalan protests in favour of Rovira's plan which was favoured more because of its local origins than because of its merits.

Cerdà's plan consisted of a square grid 133 m × 133 m (three blocks every 400 m) with 20 m wide streets, 10 m for pedestrians and 10 m for vehicular traffic. Upon this grid, tilted at 45° to the meridian to obtain the maximum sunlight, he superimposed a series of wider access routes that would link the city with its territorial environs. Unlike Rovira's plan, this scheme does not contain any obvious cultural references, but is more pragmatic, both in its geometry and in its sociological awareness of urban necessities. Geometrically, the angles of each island block are cut off, chamfered at 45°, to form octagonal squares with 20 m façades at each street intersection. Cerdà introduced this form to allow for the turning circles of public transport vehicles (he envisaged steam tramways) and space for loading and unloading goods. He planned for only two parallel buildings on each block, 20-40 m deep, with gardens in between, laced with pedestrian paths across the middle that linked each 'island' together, independent of the street network. He also planned for arranging the buildings at right-angles to each other in one corner of the 'island', and sometimes on three sides, so that by a series of combinations he could provide for macroblocks for strategic inclusion of business, administrative or service centres, or for large public parks.

In terms of social plan, the city was to be divided into two sectors of 20 × 20 (400) islands for each hospital, large park, etc. Each of these sectors was to be subdivided into four districts of 10 × 10 (100) islands for each market, and these districts further subdivided into four neighbourhoods each for schools, social centres, etc. There was, therefore, no main centre, and even the old city was treated as part of the new one, suggested by the opening up of at least three major streets orthogonal to the grid plan. Buildings were to be limited in height to five floors, spreading the population out to achieve a density of only 250 habitants per hectare. What was proposed was in effect a garden city, with public rather than private gardens, resembling Thomas Cubbitt's Bloomsbury squares in London.

Cerdà's plan for Barcelona was the first formal step, and a giant one, towards a Modern Catalonia, free from historical references, designed for a new society. While accepting the formal concept of urban life, he mellowed it with the infiltration of a network of public gardens, decades before Ebenezer Howard proposed his own versions of the garden city in 1898. Cerdà's plan, however, was ill-received by the city fathers, who preferred the grandeur of Rovira's plan, and by the landowners who saw their speculation severely limited. And it was the latter which has prevented us from experiencing Cerdà's vision today. The islands have been built up along all four sides, with deeper and higher buildings, and the majority of the interior courts filled with warehouses and other commercial buildings. The architect Puig i Cadafalch was later to remark ironically that 'the Cerdà plan was better than its development'. Once the sourness caused by the political imposition of Cerdà by Madrid had worn off, and when the economy permitted, the city was extended enthusiastically. The first residential constructions, dating from 1863, are to be found at the crossing of Roger de Llúria and Consell de Cent streets. The façades follow a simplified pattern of diminishing balcony windows from floor to floor, inspired by the pattern of neo-classical buildings in the old city. Cerdà's plan, of course, was difficult to accept, occurring as it did, like so many works of genius, ahead of or outside its time. What was a neo-classical plan doing here in what most people would understand to be the final years of Romanticism? The problem lies not so much with Cerdà himself as with the meaning we force on to words when we use them to classify and synthesize cultural history. Cerdà's plan is neo-classic in its spartan simplicity and obvious rejection of the Baroque concept of the city. But it is at the same time Utopian in its bold scientific projection into the future, while its understanding of urban sociology can be qualified as 'realist'. Moreover, the awareness of the profound influence upon society of the city form itself relates closely to the idea of a new architecture for a new civilization. There comes into view the belief that an original form could itself have both

Joan Martorell, Church of the Salesians, 1882-1885.

Antoni Rovira – Josep Fontserè – Josep Cornet, Born Market, 1873-1876.

Josep Fontserè, Plant House, 1883-1888.

'political' and spiritual significance. And this is, after all, a defining feature of Romanticism, which was capable of embracing 'suitable' forms, be they medieval or neo-classical, in the pursuit of such transcendental objectives. What we cannot accuse Cerdà of is looking back into the past for a model, unless (and we have no evidence) we think of the classical cities of the Roman colonies based on the Assyro-Babylonian *cosmopolis* like Alexandria, or the theoretical study, particularly as regards orientation, of Vitruvius. What we do have in Cerdà's plan is a highly personal work, the essential message of which is impersonal, that is to say social. The same paradox would inhabit the basic framework of Barcelona architecture for both the Romantics and the Moderns.

While Cerdà was drawing up his plan for Barcelona its citizens celebrated the first poetic and literary festival of the *Jocs Florals*, reviving the medieval conventions of the *Gaia Ciència* and thereby the status of Catalan as a language of high culture. Behind all the artificiality and the romantic nostalgia, what was reflected was a growing awareness among the elite of an interrupted tradition that involved not only its language but its institutions. In this way the past was reconnected with the present within a collective search for identity and within a gathering consciousness of 'nationhood'. In this the Catalan bourgeoisie were in line with Romantic nationalism in Europe as a whole, in that process of self-definition and revaluation of the present in terms of the past. The inherent traditionalism of the movement, aimed at recovering a lost inheritance, was initially subordinated to the immediate revolutionary implications. In Catalonia this long awakening is referred to as the *Renaixença* (Rebirth), associated with the name of the journal which, from 1871, gave expression to the original Romantic ideology of this first phase of collective revival.

The first architect of importance of the early Ro-

Lluís Domènech i Montaner, Editorial Montaner i Simon, 1880.

Josep Fontserè, Reservoir Building, section, 1874-1880.

Josep Fontserè, Reservoir Building, ground plan, 1874-1880.

mantic period was Elies Rogent (1821-1897), who as a student in 1845 publicly burnt his copy of Vignola's classical manual. He had already travelled to Paris, Munich, Berlin and other European cites to see for himself the latest buildings by the masters of the Romantic movement. He was particularly influenced by the German *Rundbogenstil*, the round-arched style of Leo von Klenze, Ludwig Persius, Von Gärtner and others, especially the university buildings in Munich erected between 1816 and 1852. In 1860 Rogent was commissioned to design the new university building of Barcelona, which was originally to have been sited within the old city but which was eventually, in consultation with Cerdà himself, assigned to a prominent place in the *Eixample* or new extension. The building is based on the strong container of neoclassical design, but its appearance is styled following the *Rundbogenstil*, appropriate not only in its cosmopolitan modernity but also in responding to the rich archaeological and architectural inheritance of Catalonia, the Romanesque, which stirred the imagination of those searching the past for points of reference in a renewal of national identity. Indeed, only four years later Rogent was appointed to restore the Romanesque abbey of Ripoll. On the other hand, as a follower of Viollet-le-Duc, he left the iron columns of the university library exposed, even though we must interpret this now more as a willingness to incorporate and expose new materials for a chosen style than as a step towards a radically modern architecture. The internal planning of the university is somewhat chaotic, as he tried to accommodate the brief into his preconceived building container. The plans were finally completed in 1868 and the building finished in 1872. It is thus in more than one sense a solid piece of history.

Rogent became the first head of the new school of architecture in 1875 and exercised a profound influence on the new generations by rejecting

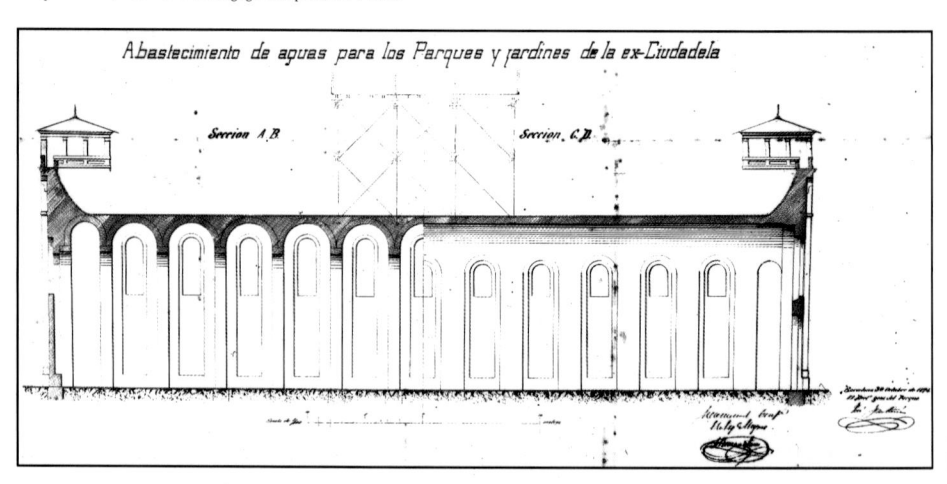

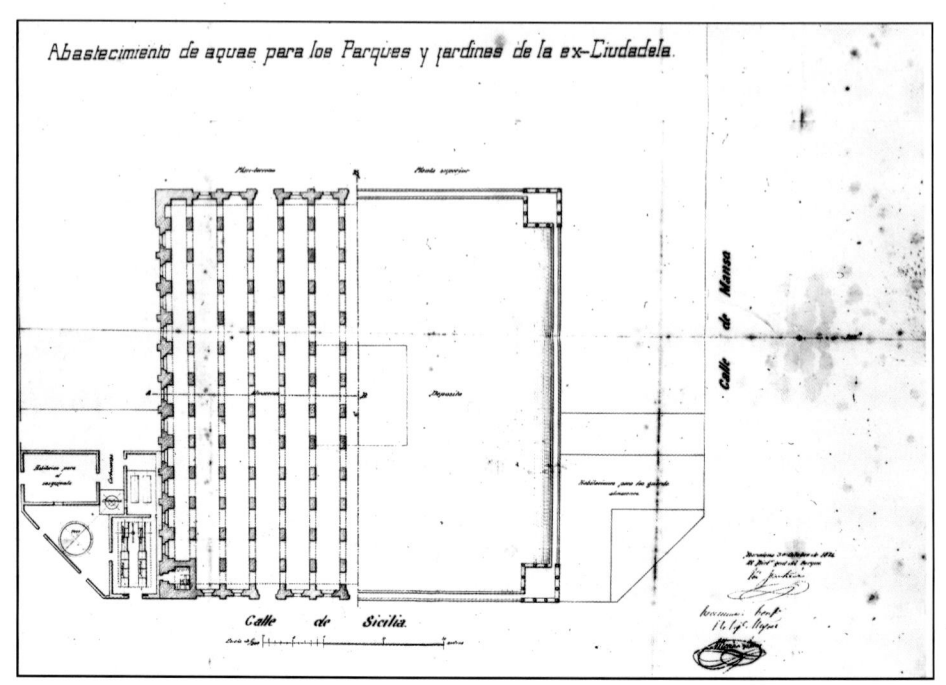

Josep Fontserè, Reservoir Building, 1874-1880 (restored in 1988 by Ignacio Paricio, Lluís Clotet and Joan Sabater).

the classical teaching of the old *Llotja*, the official school of fine arts. He encouraged a deliberate eclecticism, treating all historical periods as valid sources for formal design, an eclecticism whose presence would continue to be felt as a distinctive characteristic of Catalan architecture well into the twentieth century. Indeed, one could say that eclecticism emerged here to constitute a major and definitive characteristic of architectural Modernism in Catalonia.

As head of the school Rogent was invited to direct the buildings for the 1888 Universal Exhibition where he did much to promote the younger generation. The exhibition, in fact, marks the watershed between the works of the early Romantics, like Rogent himself, and the rising generation that was to create a radical and distinctively Catalan modern architecture, the architecture of *Modernisme*.

From among the early Romantic contemporaries of Rogent, we find Josep Oriol Mestres (1815-1895) and August Font (1846-1924) building an academic neo-gothic façade for Barcelona cathedral between 1887 and 1889 on a competition project won in 1857. Joan Martorell (1833-1906) built his neo-gothic brick and glazed-tiled church of Saint Francesc de Sales, completed in 1885. The four earliest works of Antoni Gaudí (1852-1926) —the *Casa Vicens* (1883-1885); *El Capricho* (1883-1885) in Comillas, Santander; the crypt of the *Sagrada Família* (1883-1893); the gate and pavillions for the Güell estate in Pedralbes (1887) — are all neo-medieval in their function and articulation, with prominent Arab or oriental features in their decoration. Lluís Domènech i Montaner (1850-1923) and Josep Vilaseca (1843-1910) working together produced a series of mannered eclectic designs which included an influential competition project for a large secondary educational building that was never built. Separately, in 1874, Domènech designed a quieter neo-romanesque façade, retaining some of the mannerism of his work with Vilaseca, for the publishing house of Montaner i Simon in the Carrer d'Aragó (1880). Vilaseca remained the eclectic *par excellence*. His *Tallers Vidal* (1879-1884) have a strong oriental or Egyptian influence, which is even more apparent in his house in the Rambla for Bruno Cuadros (1885) and the Batlló tomb (1885) in the Montjuïc cemetery.

The Balaguer museum and library in Vilanova i La Geltrú (1882) by Jeroni Granell (1834-1889), with its battered walls and robust mouldings, parallels Vilaseca's Egyptian styling. This, together with the exaggerated palm-leaf decoration over the cornices and pediments, later referred to by Domènech as the style of Lysicrates, makes this building the most Egyptian-influenced Greek monument in Catalonia! A monument also of eclecticism.

Josep Domènech i Estapà (1858-1917), on the other hand attempted to match the mood of collective confidence (and in that sense to break with the past) through an academic scientific approach. His beaux-arts monumentality, however, had an extremely conservative orientation. Part of the explanation for this undoubtedly lies in his succession of commissions for public building like the prison, law courts, gas company headquarters, the *Hospital Clínic*, Fabra Observatory, etc., which demanded a representative and symbolic architecture. His Science Academy building in the Rambla (1883) already shows signs of monumentality in the symmetrical composition of the facade and the towers above. His mannered style with its crude stripped historicism places him, albeit, ambiguously, in the past, despite his intentions and consciousness of building for a new era. His most sensitive building is precisely the Science Academy, whose firmly proportioned façade incorporates exposed terra-cotta low reliefs, instead of stone, with idyllic neo-classical motifs. Domènech i Estapà's work can be said, in a sense, to have given a Romantic context to surviving preoccupations of the Enlightenment.

Within the same period, but obviously freed from cultural connotations, we find the iron architecture of the Born market (1873-1876) by the engineer Josep Cornet (1838-1916), with the collaboration of Josep Fontserè (1829-1927), following the lay-out by the municipal architect Antoni Rovira. Similarly, the Saint Antoni market (1876-1882) is another product of collaboration, but this time between Cornet alone and Rovira. Meanwhile in 1874 Fontserè designed another fascinating industrial-like building: the massive roof-top reservoir in Carrer Wellington, which was completed in 1880.

The two most fecund buildings of this phase were without doubt Lluís Domènech's *Editorial Montaner* and Gaudí's *Casa Vicens*. The former is really a workshop with a street façade attached. Like all industrial buildings of the time, the work-space is constructed lightly with iron columns, beams and trusses, and is spread out on two floors. The internal format is reflected in the tall arcades of the façade. The upper floor, the type-setting area, is fully glazed, as is the top part of the frontage, giving the building a quite 'modern' look if we take in only this part. This functional aspect of the building —which is expressed, not disguised— sets Domènech's architecture apart from the rest of his contemporaries'. However, we should be careful not to read too much radicalism into such concepts. The façade of the publishing house is made of exposed brick, thus breaking with the classical tradition, but he has topped the window-bays with semi-circular 'romanesque' arches which refer backwards to Rogent's *Rundbogenstil* university, and beyond. Above the arches there is a laced pattern of brick, reflecting Domènech's admiration of Arab or *mudéjar* architecture as preserved in Teruel and elsewhere. Glazed ceramic tiles are also introduced, and the parapet contains the mannered ornamentation used by Vilaseca. The building, then, exploits eclecticism but tries to control it in accordance with local tradition and to adapt it to new forms determined mechanically by structural science, economics, acoustics and the client's brief. Some of the solutions arrived at in the *Editorial Montaner* were to be adumbrated theoretically in Domènech's article, 'In search of a national architecture', published in *La Renaixença* in 1878. His quite conscious concern was to link the present with the past, which it was unnatural for him to reject. Eclecticism was the key to a major transition. In this way he set himself apart from his contemporaries, for whom the eclectic vocabulary was generally more unreflecting and superficial. In his case, then we can talk of a Modern Romanticism in that the search for identity begins to be focussed on the present.

In 'In search of a national architecture' Domènech admits that it is difficult, if not impossible, to form an architectural unity that could be explicitly 'Spanish' and at the same time universally acceptable. The accidents of geology, topography and history do influence form in a 'natural' way, but above all, he asserts, architecture needs the energy of a productive idea within the society that demands, stimulates and criticizes it. While it is possible to interpret these ideas in relation to the gathering force of political Catalanism at the time, we should observe that by 'national' Domènech means 'Spanish', not 'Catalan', so he must be read with proper regard to context. Even so, a further dimension of the new awareness is evidenced in Domènech's article: the outward gaze towards contemporary Europe. The inwards gaze, the sense of local tradition remain constant and are even intensified, but they are to be tested and validated by comparison with those advanced national cultures that Catalan society is becoming increasingly capable of emulating. The travels, writings and architectural works of Domènech and others inject a fertile cosmopolitanism into the quest for identity. The idea of *modernity* itself assumes active prominence and as it does so Catalan *Modernisme* comes into being.

Antoni Gaudí hardly needs any introduction. No other architect has had so many books written about him and his work. It is necessary, though, to rectify a certain mythology which shows him as a lone genius, a revered mystic. This image derives from his later period when he was exclusively dedicated to work on the *Sagrada Família* church. A group of well-meaning collaborators have described their experience of Gaudí, and their accounts have fed this profusion of publications that cultivate the version of the architect as an 'outsider'. But it is as an 'insider' among his fellow architects that Gaudí's contribution to the modern movement really counts. He was, in fact, closely integrated with all that was going on around him, and his own professional history fits comfortably into the general lines of our story. Gaudí, like others, was caught up with the early Romantics' searching the past for a new vocabulary.

Gaudí's early work shows a disciplined control over the composition of architecture, confidently adapting the eclectic vocabulary that was developed in the transition from *Renaixença* Romanticism to the expressive personalization of *Modernisme*. The *Casa Vicens* has a hesitant symmetrical plan that hides an agile aggregation of domestic rooms. The difficulty inherent in such a combination has been superbly camouflaged in the design of the façades: a symmetrically pitched roof in the form of a *W* over a continuous gallery, combined with a gradual change in the intensity of materials, from stone rubble with brick ribbons laced with bands of green and yellow floral tiles, through to corbelled turrets over the awkward corners, give unity and apparent coherence to the house. The metalwork has its source in Viollet-le Duc, whose illustrated works were familiar to Gaudí. (The famous metal fence,

Antoni Gaudí, Casa Vicens, 1883-1885.

with its palm-leaf design, was installed at a later date.) The *Casa Vicens* already expresses what was to be Gaudí's basic approach to his work: a strong architectural idea or concept to which the plan is fitted, and careful elaboration of a decorative theme developed in the course of building, capable of concealing any inconsistencies in the original project. Architects at that time rarely drew more than the minimum amount of plans. The fact that Gaudí produced many, for his early works, would indicate that such inconsistencies were created by him out of deliberate choice, as a way of regulating the plan to the discipline of the main architectural idea.

The *Casa Vicens*, built for a tile manufacturer, is really a three-storey semi-detached (against the blind wall of a convent now demolished). In its decoration we find references to the budding Arts and Crafts movement (especially in the floral elements), to the *mudéjar* (in ornamental patterns) and to the fashionable East (in a smoking-room ceiling worthy of De Quincey's Opium Eater).

The two most original and influential features of this building are, however, the introduction of the outside room, a shuttered gallery with horizontally pivoted screens, and the double façade along the second floor where the windowed wall lies in a second plane behind the columned gallery. With the first Gaudí created the concept of an outside room, and with the second he imaginatively exposed then reconciled conflicting demands on the wall —façade composition in relation to interior function— creating a microclimatic breathing-space within the exterior wall itself. This addition to the vocabulary was later to have considerable currency in Catalan architecture. The incorporation of plant boxes, as well as the fountain, into the fabric of the house was a further innovation in the design of a home, later used extensively by the American architect Frank Lloyd Wright. What we see here is the underlining of a new and closer relationship between domestic life and the garden. If its origins can be traced back, through Nash and Repton in the early nineteenth century, to Rousseau's eighteenth-century 'naturalism', it was Gaudí, in the particular context of Barcelona, who revitalized and freshly re-projected the concept.

In one sense these two buildings, by Domènech and Gaudí, represent the culmination and the first solid success of the search for identity in the past. Domènech retrieves both the functional expression of Gothic architecture and constructive expression of a local material, brick. Gaudí retrieves from the Mediterranean tradition the frontier space between inside and outside to control the climate for comfort, while his mixing of Nature and Urbanity refers back to an idealized intimacy between the two. Both architects rely on eclectic decoration, but this is now regulated in a secondary role. Catalan architecture thus enters a new phase, of which the key-note is self-confidence.

Antoni Gaudí, Casa Vicens, 1883-1885.

Josep Vilaseca, Arc de Triomf, 1888.

II

THE MODERN ROMANTICS:
A SEARCH FOR IDENTITY IN THE PRESENT

In the long term, the fall of the first Spanish Republic in 1874 marked the end in Catalonia of 'an active alliance between progressive liberals and the local proletariat', as Salvador Giner expresses it. The Restoration period was to see Catalan working classes cultivating their own explicitly proletarian politics (including cooperative and anarchist strains), while the middle classes, in a period of relative prosperity and stability, continued to expand and increasingly to envisage their own future to lie in membership of the modern European family of national bourgeoisies. The cultural dimension of this process was to swell into the phenomenon known as *Modernisme*. It was a new wave of Catalan artists and intellectuals (characteristically the offspring of industrialists), appealing directly to the self-conscious professional classes, who affirmed a unique and autonomous cultural identity, the distinctive expression of the European and authentically *modern* characteristics of Catalan society. The movement was so powerfully motivated and so magnetic that it would even produce, over the turn of the century, an apparent rapprochement between the oligarchy and the proletariat.

In the architectural sphere, the Universal Exhibition of 1888 was a major focal point in these developments. In the immediately preceding years the Barcelona bourgeoisie had enjoyed the prosperity which had permitted a quite dramatic push forward in the building of Cerdà's *Eixample*. The purchasing power of the agricultural sector had grown largely as a consequence of the effects of phyloxera on the French wine industry; the opening of the Cuban market brought a cotton boom, while the Catalan wool industry grew rapidly to become the third largest in Europe; a new phase of railway development was undertaken; the Barcelona stock market experienced the spectacular 'Gold Fever' of 1881-1883. When the boom broke altogether in 1886, plans for the Universal Exhibition, already mooted during the earlier euphoria, were taken up as a means of smothering the shock of economic collapse and of recovering momentum. The enthusiasm of the mayor Francesc Rius i Taulet was largely responsible for making the event possible, following very closely the model of other recent international fairs. For all it was a response to temporary crisis, the Exhibition marked a new phase in the modernization of the atmosphere and aspect of Barcelona. The city was claiming for itself a prominent place on the map of Europe.

Elies Rogent was appointed as architect to manage the actual building of the Fair. The site chosen was that of the recently demolished 18th century fort, converted into a park designed by Josep Fontserè for a competition in 1873. Following Paxtons's Crystal Palace and the immense oval of the 1867 Paris exhibition, a single large pavilion was decided upon for the *Palau de la Indústria* by Jaume Gustà (1853-1936), the semicircular radial form of the building fitting well into the design of the park. Numerous other smaller buildings were distributed around this formal centre-piece of the exhibition. The event itself was an immense success, with 12,000 stands from 25 different countries, visited by over 400,000 foreigners: a truly cosmopolitan affair. The challenge presented to the architects Lluís Domènech, Josep Vilaseca and Josep Fontserè can for our purpose be seen as marking the beginning of the era of *Modernisme*.

A schematic characterization of *modernista* architecture can be established by reference to general historical currents and to a particular stylistic influence or imprint. First, the movement is located as a phase of urgent neoterism, between two other phases whose underlying legitimation tended to be drawn from the past: the *Renaixença*, with its simple romantic historicism, and *Noucentisme* (the subject of our Chapter III) with its ideal of Mediterranean classicism. In terms of style, *modernista* architecture was intimately marked by the forms and spirit of *Art Nouveau*, that pervasive international influence which, shaped by the writings of Ruskin and Morris, was exemplified in architecture in Émile Gallé's glass forms of the 1880's, in Victor Horta's work in Brussels and in Tiffany's favile glass in New York, and became a decisive fashion factor through the designs emanating from the *Art Nouveau* shop opened by Samuel Bing in Paris in 1895. It was an art of undulating lines and of a formalized decoration derived from 'Nature' and 'natural' patterns. For the architect it meant freedom, in the sense of a radical break with the compositional restrictions of institutional academic art. As well as welcoming new materials like iron and glass, it explored the experience of flowing space and changing light, both natural and artificial. But it was, above all, new. *Modernisme* certainly absorbed into the Catalan context the 'externals' of *Art Nouveau*, but the whole process of assimilation was itself energized by an ideological force that

Josep Vilaseca, Casa Pia Batlló, 1891-1896.

went much deeper. *Art Nouveau* arrived in Catalonia with appropriate connotations of modernity in a moment of cultural explosion, which accounts for its quantitative pervasion in this particular milieu. The sheer quantity of production provoked extreme limits of artistic synthesis, the refinement of a *modernista* style so fertile and prevalent that it permeates still the heart of present-day Barcelona. The city is a living witness to the energies of *Modernisme*.

Joan Lluís Marfany has stressed how *Modernisme* was 'a global process of renovation of a culture', linking the past with identity but, above all affirming universality in the present. The provincial limitations of the *Renaixença* were definitively transcended, even though there was a strong survival (and even a revival) of conservative currents as exemplified in the publication (1892) of *La tradició catalana* by the bishop of Vic, Torres i Bages, and promoted in art by the *Cercle Artístic de Sant Lluc*, (1893), conspicuously the neo-Nazarene inspired painters. Architecture, being by its nature slower than the pen to respond to change, inevitably retained such a conservative strain: the historical eclecticism of the *Renaixença* would be carried right through to the period of *Noucentisme*. But the opposing current of modernization, in the circumstances of an authentic cultural revolution, was in the ascendant, and in the works of its major exponents —Domènech, Gaudí and Puig— we find the paradigm of the new architecture.

Briefly, the main characteristics of *modernista* architecture can be summarized as follows: a concern for the total design (a sort of maternal gathering of all the other arts, in unity, to the architectural bosom); fluidity of space, especially in the use of the double façade and continuity of line; definition of aggregated elements; constructive features as the basis of ornamentation, independent of the architectural structure but often symbolic of structure; the assimilation of historicism and of the previous experience of eclecticism; and, finally, a generous allowance for bourgeois comforts, creating in turn a conspicuous domestic charm.

Before dealing with the three masters of *Modernisme* we should first examine the work of Josep Vilaseca (1848-1910). It is an interesting transitional case in which we find still unresolved a tension between the decorative use of eclectic elements culled from the past and experimentation with these same elements as a means of developing new forms for the present.

Vilaseca was a cultivated, well travelled and elegant architect who through his precise and fully detailed drawings produced an intelligent and well designed corpus of architectural work, classified stylistically by Rosemarie Bletter in the following chronological progression, '*Renaixença*, Egyptian, Neo-mudéjar, Neo-gothic, Japanese and *Modernisme*'. Neither this variegation nor the fact that Vilaseca did not achieve the quality of his famous contemporaries should lead us to undervalue the importance of his work. After collaborating with Domènech during the 1870's, he designed the factory workshop for Francisco Vidal (1879-1884), full of local details within its classical references, and the temple-like studio for the brothers Masriera (1882), still deeply imbued with *Renaixença* historical revivalism. With the Batlló tomb (1885), the *Casa Pla* (1885-1886) and the *Casa Bruno Cuadros* (1885-1895) we have a clear dominance of Egyptian influence, distantly deriving from the first oriental exoticism in France sparked off by Napoleon's expedition to Egypt, rekindled now by the Barcelona connections of Lesseps, the builder of the Suez Canal.

Vilaseca's choice of brick for his Triumphal Arch entrance to the 1888 exhibition is of fundamental importance. Although considered a 'poor' material, it was used not only by Vilaseca but also by Domènech for his restaurant, by Pere Flaqués for the agricultural pavilion, by Gaietà

Josep Vilaseca, Casa Joaquim Cabot, 1901.

Buïgas for the naval pavilion, by Josep Fontserè for his *Umbracle*, the water deposit building and elsewhere in the precinct. As well as giving unity to these diverse buildings, the selection of material also demonstrated an attitude. We have no written record but can assume safely that it was a deliberate choice to affirm the 'Spanish' quality of the exhibition, with reference to Arab or mudéjar architecture as we have seen already in Domènech and Gaudí (and affected by the same conceptual confusion apparent in Domènech's article (1878) on 'national' architecture). From this point onwards Vilaseca returned to a basically medieval vocabulary, but styled always in his own manner of freezing the form rather than letting it flow as Domènech or Gaudí did. He was nonetheless a fine designer who knew how to fashion a corner, finish a moulding, join materials and support a gallery. His detailing was refined, with all the sharp definition of his precise drawings, and we can see this in the three homes he built for the Batlló family (between 1892 and 1896) and finally in his house for Joaquim Cabot (1901-1905) where he begins to unfreeze and merges into the generalized current of *Modernisme*. Precisely because he was not in the vanguard, Vilaseca's work is interesting for what it shows of the permeation and consistency of a truly representative phase of architectural creativeness.

Lluís Domènech i Montaner (1850-1923) qualified as an architect in 1873 after studying in Madrid. His influence was considerable, not only as the designer of some of *Modernisme's* finest architecture but also as a teacher at the school of architecture (from 1877) whose director he became, first in 1900 and then again from 1905 to 1919. Through his interest in archaeology he was, as Oriol Bohigas underlines, a pioneer in 'the discovery of the stylistic foundations of a specifically Catalan art within the great works of the Romanesque and Gothic periods'. Bohigas goes on to highlight Domènech's role as a 'politi-

Lluís Domènech i Montaner, Palau de la Música Catalana, skylight, 1905-1908.

cal activist who promoted the great unifying actions of Catalanism, an architect of the most cultivated sector of the industrial bourgeoisie who anticipated the aesthetic of *Art Nouveau*... (who) emulated the English programme for the renewal of the industrial arts and adhered to an innovative rationalism that, at one and the same time, drew upon the historical reconstructions of Viollet-le-Duc (which encouraged a new attitude towards technology), the enthusiasm for new materials and the deterministic theories of functional and environmental character that started with Gottfried Semper'.

Domènech created two buildings for the Exhibition. The more spectacular was the International Hotel, five storeys high with a façade 160 m wide, constructed except for finishes in under three months, 'with a modular system based on criteria that anticipated some of the processes of industrialized construction' (Bohigas). It was taken down at the end of the Exhibition. The other building was the Café-Restaurant which survives as an almost perfect, as it were canonical, architectural specimen. The simplicity of its plan and internal volume is statically controlled by the double-leafed walls that run from corner to corner where they cross to form four towers, square in plan. The exterior walls of plain brick respond to the function of the interior structure and in their bleakness not only anticipate Berlage's Amsterdam Stock Exchange by a decade, but also, by this evaluation of the plane as a compositional element in its own right, introduce us to the language that we find far later in the architecture of De Styl, Oud, Dudok and even Mies van der Rohe. However, we should be careful about re-reading such a building from the perspective of our own time lest we throw out of focus the contemporary reality to which it belongs. This functional expression, already noted in the *Editorial Montaner*, was a means by which Domènech was able to cope with the short dead-line for designing and

*Lluís Domènech i Montaner, Palau de la Música Catalana,
1905-1908.*

Lluís Domènech i Montaner, Cafè-Restaurant staircase, 1888.

completing the building. The simple lay-out of one dining room above the other, entrance at one end and kitchens at the other, also helped to define the plainness of the design. According to Bohigas, time may not have allowed Domènech to incorporate all the decoration that he intended and even so it was not finished in time for the opening of the Exhibition. Be that as it may, the building stands out, as it was left and on its own merits, as a landmark in the history of *Modernisme* and of the Modern Movement as a whole. The simple way in which Domènech handled the exposed steel lintels in the façade and used the double walls that wrap around the major space to filter in natural light: these are just two of the many lessons that the building continues to teach us.

We move on now to consider Domènech's two major works: the *Palau de la Música Catalana* (1905-1908) and his *Hospital de Sant Pau* (1902-1910).

The *Palau de la Música* is often cited as the beginning of rationalist building in Barcelona, on account of its technological conception as a steel-framed glass box, the acoustic expertise of the total design, and the 'psychological' attention to the movements of a large number of people and to integration of audience and performance. On the other hand, the question of its decoration and its *spirit* has tended either to cause embarrassment or to be accepted, with a rather cold historicalness, as the *tour de force* of the sumptuousness to which *Modernisme* inclined. Although the rationalist aspects of the building and the demonstration of mastery of the *science* of architecture make the *Palau* a show-piece of the modern architectural heritage, its profoundly *artistic* properties are no less important when viewed in the perspective which we are taking here.

One of Romanticism's deepest currents was reasserted in Catalan *Modernisme*. Friedrich Schiller's concept of *erstarrte Musik* (coined in a

Lluís Domènech i Montaner, Cafè-Restaurant, 1888.

Lluís Domènech i Montaner, ground floor and main floor plan, 1888.

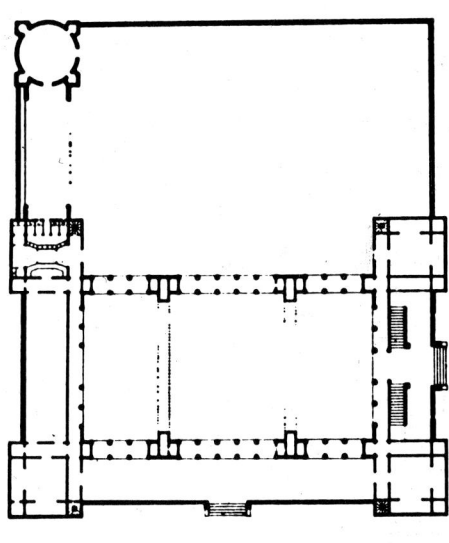

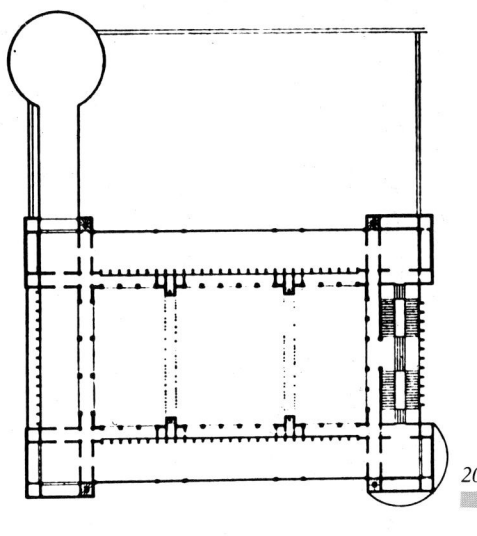

19

20

33

Lluís Domènech i Montaner, Palau de la Música Catalana, detail of the main façade, 1905-1908.

Berlin lecture in 1802) re-echoed in Lord Byron's affirmation that 'the perfection of architecture is frozen music... the perfection of beauty to my mind always present the idea of living music'. Architecture and music were thus associated, as in the painted decorations of Karl Friedrich Schinkel's *Altes Museum* in Berlin, or in his reliefs of Orpheus charming stones and Amphion building Thebes over the doorway of the Berlin School of Architecture. The same myth was referred to by both Schelling and Goethe in discussing 'frozen music'. Domènech had read his Ruskin (available to him in Catalan as well as Castilian translation) who elaborated on these concepts and who defined architecture as a 'science of feeling rather than the rule'. The Catalan architect, moreover, had many direct contacts with Germany and had experienced that wave of Wagnerism which swept over Barcelona after the performance of *Lohengrin* at the Liceu opera house in 1882. The architecture-music conjunction is proclaimed in the emerging sculptural groups of the *Palau's* proscenium: on one side, in homage to the local tradition of popular music, a bust of Anselm Clavé who instigated its revival; on the other side, in homage to the European classical tradition, Wagner's *Die Walkÿrie* cavalcade rising above the solid doric columns that frame the bust of Beethoven. This symbolism is given its nationalist reference, in characteristic *modernista* terms, in the sculptural forms by Domènech and Pau Gargallo: on one side the tree, symbol of national identity rooted in the soil, and on the other side the clouds, representing spiritual union with Europe. The very focal point of the *Palau de la Música Catalana* thus enshrines the spirit of a national culture, capable of generating its own unique and authentic expression.

Paul Scheerbart, the German contemporary of Domènech and apostle of glass architecture, would have found here the perfect exemplification of his idea of breaking loose from the en-

Lluís Domènech i Montaner, Palau de la Música Catalana, ground floor plan and concert hall plan, 1905-1908.

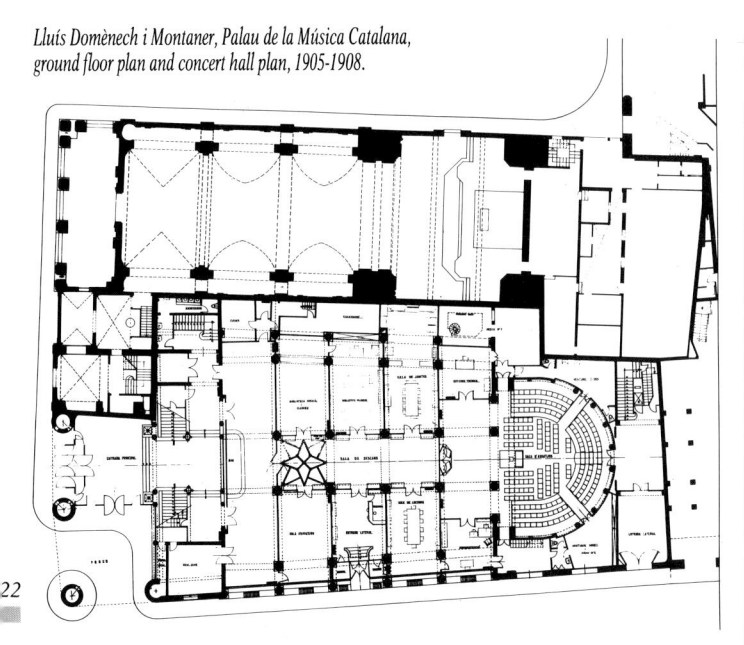

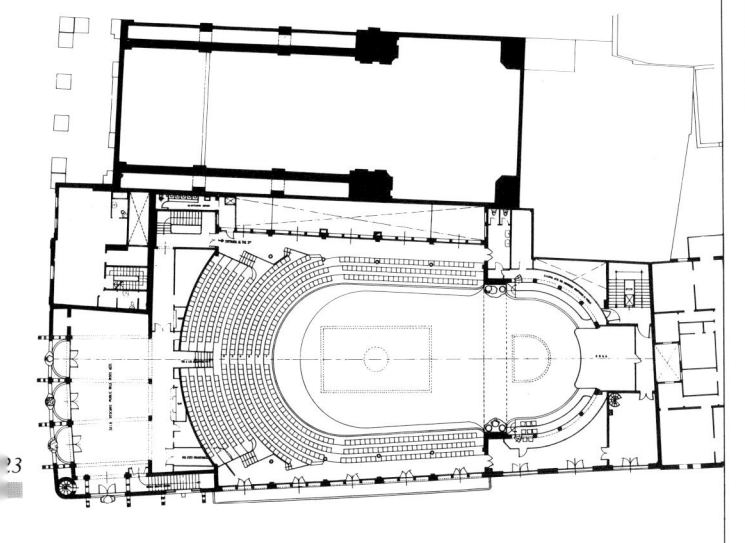

Lluís Domènech i Montaner, Palau de la Música Catalana, sculptural group by Pau Gargallo, 1905-1908.

Lluís Domènech i Montaner, Palau de la Música Catalana, main façade, 1905-1908.

*Lluís Domènech i Montaner, Hospital de Sant Pau,
a general view with one of the pavilions, 1902-1910.*

closed space with a freedom which 'lets in the sunlight' and which, with the help of iron construction, 'brings with it a new culture'. The *Palau* is a glass box within a brick cage: a cage that on this awkward street-angle site turns the corner with a majestic entrance porch and a swing of the double façade around the reception and staircase area, using as a hinge a giant sculptural group by Miquel Blay. The pattern of the brick cage changes where the main space of the concert hall begins, repeating that constant functional expression of the façade as devised by Domènech in his earlier *Editorial Montaner*. Glass is also used freely within to subdivide the areas while allowing a visual flow to permeate the whole structure. This not only enhances the unity of the building but also allows the maximum functional use of those areas which can be absorbed into each other when necessary. It is a development on from the glass screens which were used in his earlier *Fonda España* (1902-1903). In the auditorium itself the integration of performers and audience is brought about by turning around behind the scenic apse both the structure of the glass façade and the public gallery itself, creating an almost arena-stage effect. The back wall of the stage contains eighteen muses of music in a combination of Lluís Bru's graphic mosaics of dresses from different countries and Eusebi Arnau's sculptures of busts and instruments emerging from the wall. The universality of music provided the ideal analogue of that universality sought by *Modernisme* to express the ambition of the Catalan bourgeoisie that their national identity and culture should be recognized by other nations. The 'frozen music' of Domènech became its culminating expression in architecture.

Domènech's other great building, the *Hospital de Sant Pau*, is a large complex, like all such institutions, and occupies four blocks of Cerdà's city plan. But the architect broke with Cerdà's orthogonal straight-jacket and swung his building around through 45° to face south, partly for hygienic reasons and partly to express the autonomous unity of the group within the Barcelona grid. The unusual ordering of the building, in addition to its angling, introduces a further tipological innovation, as Oriol Bohigas has pointed out: 'Pavilions isolated among gardens, beneath which is organized, underground, the entire unified operation of services.' Domènech's originality here lay in the resolve with which he rejected the inhuman mass of the vast institutional building, currently in vogue for its supposed efficiency. Instead he placed major importance on the human scale of the cottage hospital, making each ward a self-contained, single-storey pavilion close to the ground and to the gardens. Apart from providing an ingenious system of permanent natural ventilation, Domènech here also applied his belief that the fresh air and other ideals of the garden city were even more important to the sick than to the healthy.

The Pere Mata mental hospital near Reus (1897-1919) is another important institutional work by Domènech. At the same time, in domestic architecture, he was working on the beautifully designed Lleó Morera house (1905), where a surviving eclectic note is subordinated to demonstration of the primacy of the façade in total composition, and the *Casa Fuster* (1908-1910) in which, as Bohigas notes, 'the graphic quality reaches a simplification such that the traditional elements — columns, capitals, cornices — lose their historic meaning and acquire the value of a simple allusion to established codes, adopting thereby a subversive attitude in regard to tradition and convention'.

As we have already suggested, Lluís Domènech's architectural work cannot be considered in isolation from his cultural and civic activities. Archaeology not only developed his close interest in ancient buildings (notably the monastery of Poblet) but also in ceramic tiles and heraldry (used in the *Fonda España*) which grew into a major private collection at his castle-like home in Canet. His academic influence was considerable. He founded in 1889, with Antoni Gallissà, a workshop of decorative arts housed in the Restaurant del Parc, which functioned till Gallissà's early death in 1903. Later, as head of the school of architecture (1900-1919) he transformed the provincial, neo-medieval and eclectic legacy of the previous director, Francesc Villar (author of the first project for the *Sagrada Família* temple), into a much more modern, cosmopolitan approach. Domènech further contributed to this broadening of the horizons of architecture with the pioneer *Historia general del Arte* (1886-1907) which he edited with the important collaboration of Puig i Cadafalch. In politics, with a strong sense of civic responsibility he was three times elected president of the Barcelona *Ateneu*, was president of the *Jocs Florals* in 1895 and for short while a prominent member of the political party *Lliga Regionalista* born of a fragile pact between conservatives and liberals. He presided over the Manresa assembly (1892) which provided the political base for a unified political nationalism. He was one of the four Catalanist MPs elected to the Madrid parliament in 1901 representing the distinctively nationalist posture adopted in this crucial period. In the ferment of early 20th-century Catalan politics he broke with the conservative *Lliga* and, in 1904, helped to found the weekly (later a daily) *El Poble Català* which became the breeding ground of the future party of *Esquerra Catalana*. This multiple activity describes the man and points to his exceptional organizing abilities. He relied on many collaborators, and was able to inspire effective teamwork as decisively in architecture as in politics. What is interesting is that there was a stock of potential collaborators upon which Domènech could draw to carry through his projects. This in itself was a sign of the extent to which *Modernisme* had achieved the relative normalization of Catalan cultural life, in the

Lluís Domènech i Montaner, Casa Lleó Morera, 1905.

sense of uniting a communal cause with a widely accepted, dynamic mode of expression. Domènech's own participation in this total movement clearly reveals the interaction of its essential ingredients: the appreciation of an historical legacy combined with the urge to be abreast of modern European fashion; this fertile mixture eagerly fostered by the consumerism and the patriotism of an enthusiastically *catalanista* bourgeoisie; the excitement of creating the visual expression of what was perceived as a new era, corroborating Jaume Brossa's prophetic slogan, 'A èpoques noves, formes d'art noves.'

The creative imagination of Antoni Gaudí (1852-1926) provided an extreme Baroque formulation of the effervescence generated by *Modernisme*. Extending the analogy, we can see in Gaudí's exuberant *Modernisme* a sort of collective Orphism of the Catalan community seeking to recover its Eurydice back across those centuries of decadence when the full experience (social and cultural) of the Baroque was denied to them. This may be one explanation for the apparent contradiction between the normal sobriety of Catalan architecture and the public acceptance of the 'exorbitance', as Nikolaus Pevsner puts it, of Gaudí's work. The contradiction itself is perhaps indicative of the gap in Catalan cultural development which Gaudí's creations bridged and closed.

In his early works, as we have seen, Gaudí maintained a disciplined control over composition in architecture. This is clearly evident in the *Palau Güell* (1885-1889), where the central hall betrays its origins in the concept of a covered court. The other rooms are placed around this court as if they had been added in an almost extemporized way. Some rather brusque constructional transitions indicate that the architect probably had to cope with last-minute changes demanded by the client as building work progressed. Analysis of the structure shows Gaudí to be a master in de-

Lluís Domènech i Montaner, Casa Fuster, 1908-1910.

ploying the arch and the vault, somewhat brutal with his steelwork and frankly unsound as to the stable limits of load-bearing walls, subjected here to stresses than run very closely the risk of buckling. The street and interior façades evidence meticulous care in the drawing stage: the former responds to the restrictions of a narrow street with a double façade, to protect the intimacy of the inside and enrich the spatial transition of light. The parabolic arch of the entrance and the rich texture of its wrought-iron gate demonstrate Gaudí's creative ability in experiments with form. The rather severe Scottish-baronial façade of the interior is a relaxed expression of the internal functions, held together by the rather forced symmetry of the tribune. Out on the roof the architect worked with a freer hand, and his chimneys and ventilation shafts, curiously out of scale with the rest of the building, give us the first display of the full range of Gaudí's original and exciting fantasies in form, material and colour.

Other important early works are the gatehouse and stables for Güell, in Pedralbes (1887), the *Col·legi Santa Teresa* (1889-1894) and the *Bellesguard* house (1900-1902). The Güell gatehouse and stables (1887) illustrate how Gaudí could lift a simple building into the realm of creative architecture without abandoning appropriately cheap materials and construction methods. The stables themselves are roofed with staggered tile vaults (the Catalan vault, a legacy of the Romans, consisting of two or three layers of overlapping tiles glued together in quick-setting cement in a curved vault form that is initiated from the supporting wall or arch without the normal shuttering for its temporary support). These are supported by wafer-thin brick parabolic arches between each stable. The square exercise room has a vault sitting on simple squint arches. In these two buildings, together with the forged iron dragon gate, we see a Gaudí feeling his way towards a refinement of local construction and a distinctive richness of compositional decoration, both of which predominate strongly over the marked touches of Arabic patterns and other eclectic details.

The Col·legi de Santa Teresa convent is Gaudí's most severe rational building, simple and economical, with decoration limited to an expression of construction and to control over the horizontal composition of the façade with a richer line of recessed pointed openings, both blind and real, along the upper fourth floor. This nuns' residence, for which the aspect as well as the reality of economy was required, disciplined Gaudí to produce a strict rectangular building (60 m × 18 m) of four storeys. Within, it has a staggered linear light-well, running along the major axis, with corridors on either side. Buckling of the lengthy internal walls is avoided by twisting the first-floor wall to accommodate lateral fins pierced by parabolic arches. The majestic simplicity of form and structure is evocative of the great pragmatic civic tradition in Catalan architecture, found in its late medieval stock exchanges, civic halls and religious buildings.

The *Bellesguard* house completes this trio of buildings which show us a Gaudí doing ordinary work extraordinarily well. *Bellesguard* is a formal exercise in the unity of material to match the ruins of the nearby castle, with stone facing on roof and walls, and even on the drain pipes. But the study under the roof, with its dextrously thin arched cantilevers in brick, strikingly abuses structural economy not only for decoration but also for spatial effects that are quite absorbing. No doubt there are simpler ways of building: Gaudí in his prime seems to have delighted in creating problems in order to demonstrate how he could solve them. The results are of exceptional interest, for they present a paradigm of the role of that redundant design in architecture which the Rationalism of some thirty years later would contest so rigorously. Seen in its immediate context, though, the compact plan of *Bellesguard* reminds one of Gaudí's contemporary C.F.A. Voysey whose work, including Perrycraft in Malvern (1893-1894), was widely published in *The Studio* and broadcast in Europe and America through the writings of the Belgian Van de Velde. The kinship extends as far as Frank Lloyd Wright's Winslow house in Chicago, likewise distinguished by its compact plan and emphasis on horizontal lines. It was at this point in his career that Gaudí himself departed from this simplifying process of formal synthesis, the line that was carried on by Mackintosh, Olbrich, Behrens, Hoffman and Lutyens abroad, and by Domènech, Puig, Berenguer, Muncunill, Jujol and Masó at home. A sudden increase in commissions around 1900, and no doubt increasing confidence, led Gaudí to evolve his design methods through sketches and models, which were a more appropriate means of composing his architecture around a strong central idea. There are interesting correspondences between the poet Maragall's theory of inspired expression based upon *la paraula viva* (the living word) and Gaudí's contemporary effort to give architectural shape to the creative process itself. Thus, the oval plan of the crypt of the chapel in the *Colònia Güell*, gathering the congregation around the altar; the integration of nature and architecture in the *Parc Güell;* the flowing form of the Batlló house, based on the theme of St George and the Dragon; *La Pedrera* or *Casa Milà*, luxury apartments in a free plan made possible by the use of a stone hung-curtain wall on a steel frame; the structural form of the school buildings of the *Sagrada Família* temple; and, finally, the tapering cylindrical towers of the *Sagrada Família* itself: this is the compendium of Gaudí's unique contribution to *Modernisme*, and of that unmistakable 'Baroque' effusion from which his name is inseparable.

The previous allusion to Maragall has already indicated Gaudí's filiation with a pronounced

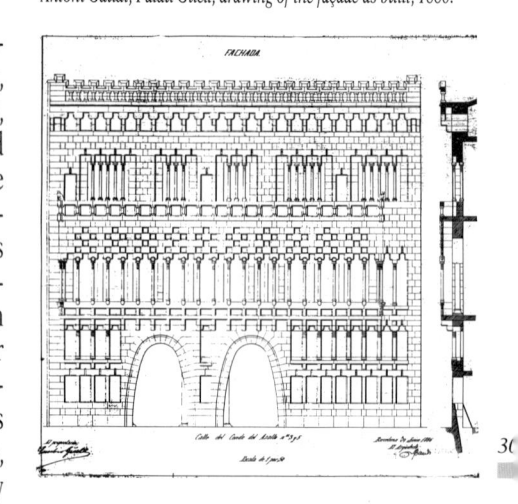

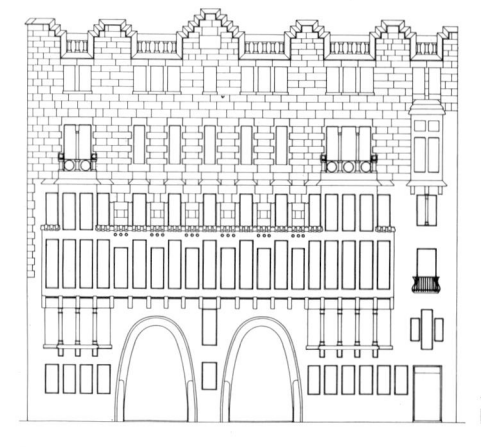

Antoni Gaudí, Palau Güell, project of the façade, 1886.

Antoni Gaudí, Palau Güell, drawing of the façade as built, 1886.

Antoni Gaudí, Palau Güell, 1885-1889.

Antoni Gaudí, Casa Calvet, 1899.

neo-romantic tendency in *Modernisme*, particulary as regards the exaltation of individual artistic inspiration. As with the architecture-music analogy in the case of Domènech, the architecture-poetry motif has very deep roots in Romantic theory. Carl Menzel wrote in 1832: 'A piece of architecture in which there are any manifestations of genius is worked out in the same manner as a poem: invention, or the ground idea of the subject, must come first, and it is to this conception of the fancy that technical skill is afterwards applied, so as to work it up and render practicable in construction what is originally the mere apprehension of beauty. This is the only true process.' The same idea is the basis of Ruskin's architecture/building, poetry/verse distinction as elaborated in *The Stones of Venice*, a work which was available in translation to the Catalan architects and artists and which was a typical influence in the formation of *modernista* aesthetics.

It is nevertheless important to understand Gaudí's role in the creation of his major works as that of a determined and persistent creator, holding to and developing a single architectural purpose (or 'invention') through the mediation of his team of collaborators, ranging from the precise sobriety of Berenguer to the rococo graphics of Jujol. In addition to these close assistants, Gaudí also gathered around him able craftsmen and artists who, completely identified with the spirit of *Modernisme*, were able to add their own contributions to the master's overall vision. Architecture being a preeminently practical art-form, Gaudí's 'poetic' genius both thrived in and inspired this kind of operational teamwork.

The crypt chapel in the *Colònia Güell* (1898-1915) is comparable in concept only whith Le Corbusier's Ronchamp Chapel (1950-1954). Both break with the traditional basilican plan and adopt a more Baroque spatial scheme, but Gaudí's design is in some ways more audacious on account of the hardly perceptible double aisle and the continuation of the choir gallery behind the central altar literally gathering the enclosed space around it. With great sensitivity to the personal dimension of a Christian gathering, where human contacts can prolong the spiritual ones, he extended the shelter of his chapel with a lowering porch tilted towards the sun and forming a breezeway that mingles with the surrounding pine-wood, so that one is comfortably and ambiguously both inside and outside the church at the same time. With a sort of 'gentleman's agreement' that removes uncomfortableness, Gaudí has acknowledged the fact that men tended traditionally to hover close to the church entrance with the womenfolk converged on the service inside. This layered entry, like the double façades, is picked up with the suggestion of two aisles that swing around the altar inside the chapel. The exterior stone wall is extraordinarily thin, almost literally folded, as though it were paper, to gain the necessary strength for stability (an idea that was to be exploited by Marcel Breuer in his UNESCO building in Paris, completed in 1958). We can now see that Gaudí was here confronting one of the major problems of 20th-century architecture, that is the question of thin walls and the associated violence of the transition between outside and inside. One of Gaudí's solutions, anticipating the ideas of Louis Kahn in the 1960's, was to thicken out the wall around the window reveals, thus allowing the introduction of a frame of coloured tiles that could soften the reflected light upon the coloured glazing. Apart from this and many other sensitive details, perhaps the most surprising thing is the placing of the chapel in relation to the formal axial planning of the colony of worker's housing in the total complex of the *Colònia Güell* by Gaudí, Berenguer and Rubió, constructed after the completion of the new Güell and Alsina factory between 1891 and 1912. At one end of the village is Berenguer's school, in the centre

Antoni Gaudí, Santa Teresa Convent, 1889-1894.

34

the main square, and at the other end one would expect the church, as was done in Port Sunlight (1887) for instance: but no, Gaudí placed his chapel casually off away from any dominant position, on the wooded hillside nearby, thus bringing religion into communion with nature. The full church building that was originally projected was never completed, perhaps fortunately if we are to judge from the surviving sketches and inverted model (and from the imprecision of his design ideas of later years). Obsessed at this time with how to continue the neo-gothic crypt of the *Sagrada Família* with a more scientifc solution to the outward thrust of the vaults, Gaudí profited from the mathematical and constructive talents of Joan Rubió (collaborating between 1893 and 1906) to study the form of the chapel that should occur from a mechanical or 'natural' distribution of the weight of the roof. This was ingeniously done by inverting a model made of canvas slung between cables supporting tiny sacks of sand, rather like a mobile sculpture. It was an attempt to find form through structure that was obviously subject to a preconceived idea about the image of the required building. Even so it was a method of design which clearly contributed in a practical way to the final symmetrical form of a centralized plan. Further, a natural consequence of this experimental design process was the improvization that ensued during the construction itself. It is obvious that the almost anarchic tracery of the brick arches and ribs that spring from the tilted columns could never have been drawn. The crypt of the chapel took shape, in fact, like a full-scale model, which needed almost daily supervision. Gaudí had a good team to support him in this, notably Berenguer and, at different times, Rubió and Jujol. Indeed, the undertaking was effectively terminated with Berenguer's death in 1914. Although there is speculation about how the completed building might have looked, the fact is that continuation of the chapel might well have meant destruction of the seminal architectural model that we are left with. A product still of the discipline carried over from his early work, but already incorporating his personal Baroque feeling for space, the crypt of the *Colònia Güell* must be considered Gaudí's finest work.

In the *Parc Güell* (1900-1914) Gaudí brought his architecture even closer to nature. His client, Eusebi Güell, was one of the most powerful members of the Catalan industrial bourgeoisie. Married into the aristocratic family of the Comillas, Güell had important business contacts in England and France which gave him both the wealth and the cultural outlook to make him one of the outstanding patrons of modern architecture. It is related that Gaudí first came to his notice as the designer of a stand for the glove firm Comella in the Paris exhibition of 1878. After the stables, the Count's own house and the chapel for his worker's village, Gaudí now applied himself to giving shape to the ideas acquired by his patron in England for a 'garden city' and to designing the infrastructure of a small privileged community on one of the hillsides overlooking Barcelona. The *Parc Güell* is distinctly Arcadian in conception: the placing of the Calvary high up on a rock outcrop seems deliberately to evoke C.D. Friedrich's well-known painting *The Cross in the Mountain* (1807-1808) and the iconography of a whole tradition of Romantic landscape painting that it inspired. Seen in this light, Gaudí's park can be interpreted as a counterpart in building of this pictorial mode. The grotto-like passages and bridges recreate Rousseaunian images of the bosom of nature while classical motifs of the Golden Age are recalled in the ironic use of the Doric columns for the market under the square in the middle of the park. Around the edge of this raised square we find the famous curved tile bench which snakes its way from one side to the other. What appears to be a free form is actually a composition of prefabricated curved and countercurved pieces which match the geometry of the market hall below. Nor is it gratuitously decorative: its sinuous shape, comfortably designed to accommodate the human figure, presents the alternative opportunity of sitting facing other people, thereby becoming part of a group, or of facing away, enjoying the freedom to be alone in a crowd. It is the same insight into 'social' behaviour that Gaudí displayed in the layered entry and the benches of his *Colònia Güell* chapel. The *trencadís* or broken tilework covering the seats is a spectacular performance in a collage technique that anticipates aspects of modern abstract geometrical patterning. It has something, too, of a surrealistic revaluation of commonplace objects, lovingly set out by J.M. Jujol who was obviously developing another of Gaudí's ideas. Below the square and market, like sentinels on either side of the entrance gate, are two Disney-like lodges, the most interesting feature of which is the fact that Gaudí has realized that their roofs are effectively a fifth façade, being moulded and tiled as such and forming a delightful sight from above. These were, however, the only houses to be built, except for one by Berenguer which now contains a small Gaudí museum. With the death of Güell in 1918 the garden-city idea lost its prime mover and the grounds were shortly afterwards sold to the city to become a public park.

The *Casa Batlló* (1905-1907) in the Passeig de Gràcia was a conversion of an existing house which Gaudí 'modernized' with an impressive face-lift. Evelyn Waugh, writing about it in the *Architectural Review* of 1930, mistook it for something to do with the Turkish Consulate, so exotic did he find this building. Even today it is certainly an odd-looking construction. The *Casa Batlló*, nevertheless, has two major lessons to teach us, one inside and the other outside. The central court has been reformed so that its staggered section opens out as it reaches up-

Antoni Gaudí, Casa Batlló, 1905-1907.

Antoni Gaudí, Casa Milà (La Pedrera – The stone quarry), 1905-1911.

Antoni Gaudí and Josep Maria Jujol, Casa Milà, a detail of the ceiling, 1905-1911.

Antoni Gaudí, Casa Milà, a detail of the staircase, 1905-1911.

wards (as in the Convent of Santa Teresa), the window sizes grow as they descend, and the coloured tiles change gradually from all white to blue between the bottom and the topmost floor. Gaudí realized that a multi-storey apartment building does not just consist of one equal dwelling placed on top of another, and here he accordingly took account of each unit's differing relationship with the light-well. The façade has a similar composition, with wide bulging openings creating a double façade on the first floor which Gaudí completely reformed for the owners. The original window openings were retained as a base for the composition, only the top left-hand room being removed, demolished by Gaudí in order to tie up with Puig's *Casa Amatller* next door: an extraordinary example of good manners in urban architecture, seldom, if ever, seen nowadays. Now, as the house faces S.E. it catches only the early-morning sun and then only at an angle. In order to enliven this façade Gaudí introduced an undulating skin across the surface which he faced with *trencadís*, broken tiles and plates, etc., in a delicately coloured texture which reflects the early-morning sunlight and contrasts with the muscular stone awnings and bone-like pillars of the lower tribunes. Moreover, Gaudí gave free rein here to his desire to stamp each building with his personal signature and wit. In this case he went to the extent of impregnating the whole façade with a symbolic 'poster' of national identity incorporating that most potent of Catalonia's collective emblems, Saint George. The patron saint is illustrated here with the presence of his lance, a small turret crowned with a cross, piercing the tile-scaled dragon's back of the roof, beneath which we find the metal balconies shaped to form the skulls and bones of the victims. The confidence of genius (and the receptivity of a politically galvanized cultural ethos) is needed for this kind of positive flouting of all the conventions of architectural connotation.

The *Casa Milà* or *La Pedrera* (1905-1911), on the other side of the Passeig de Gràcia, is a much larger building and contains several advanced innovations. Here Gaudí used a steel-frame structure in order to free the layout of each floor from the normal restrictions of load-bearing walls. Where previously steel structures had merely replaced conventional walls, here Gaudí realized that he was now free to bend them at will. This differential layered composition of the plan is expressed in the same differential layering of the facade. Gaudí simply hung his bush-hammered stone curtain upon the steel structure, in the same way that our business buildings have their glass façades hung. In the process of doing this he subjected the design of the steel structure to his idea of free planing in such a way that many of the columns do not coincide with the ones below. The medium bestows this freedom: Gaudí was the first to exploit it. Another innovation was to separate the lifts from the staircases. Since the introduction of mechanical lifts, architects had limited themselves to adding a lift-shaft to the staircase. Gaudí realized that by separating the two he could vary access to the apartments and at the same time relegate the stairs to use by servants. Large apartment dwellings could thus be designed according to the traditional hierarchy of the detached house, without problems of cross-circulation between owners and servants. Two other innovations were: first, the acceptance of the carriage or motor-car within the building, allowing it to be driven into the courtyard and then, by way of a spiral ramp, to be parked underground; secondly, the recovery of the roof as a public space for use by the inhabitants. The building exceeds considerably the normal height of its contemporary neighbours, so to dissimulate this dubious excess Gaudí covered the sloping façades of the upper floors with white tiles which merge in tone with the sky. To the observer the main visual impact of *La Pedrera* comes not from such innovations but from the impressive wave-like rhythms of the irregular façade walls draped with sea-weedy balconies. The constant movement of the composition evokes at once Van Gogh's idea of the 'caricature of the real' in art and also something akin to the impact sought by the expressionists. Illustrations in the contemporary satirical journal, *Cu-Cut!* and *L'Esquella de la Torratxa*, ridiculing Gaudí's *Casa Milà*, would indeed indicate quite a deep affinity of purpose and effect —a deliberate shock to the complacent bourgeois— between the *Modernista* architect's 'expressionism' and the *frisson* of Edvard Munch's famous lithograph *The Cry* (1893).

Certainly, Gaudí broke clean away from the classical disciplines of architecture and created a personal style that gave a novel interpretation to the concept of the Baroque. The results could have been chaotic, were it not for the strength of his imposed ideas which gave unity to each of his compositions. The common elements in Gaudí's Baroque manner are the attention to human circumstances and the constructional basis of many of his most original details and effects, which he infused with a considerable humour. If his wit is something which helps us to enjoy his buildings, it must also have sustained Gaudí himself, and his creativity, during the laborious process of work on each project and construction of each building. The enigma of Gaudí is that, although he was an outstanding talent, he failed to consolidate a viable architectural discipline that could be continued and elaborated by his followers. His abundant imagination, private wit and public self-confidence finally became mortgaged to a consuming and reactionary religiosity that grew up around him through his work on the *Sagrada Família* temple. He misread his brief, and it destroyed him. His architecture became subjected to a religion of symbols. After 1914, with the Catalan cultural elite rejecting the 'chaos' of *Modernisme* in favour of the classic order of Mediterranean culture, disoriented by the death of his patron Güell and of his chief assistant Berenguer, Gaudí withdrew more and more into his private obsessions. It is from this later phase, as we have remarked previously, that the myth of Gaudí derives. The foregoing pages have been concerned with demonstrating the relevance and centrality of his work within the whole dynamism of Catalan *Modernisme*. Seen in this light, the achievements and the contradictions of the architect manifest their true significance.

Josep Puig i Cadafalch (1867-1956), fifteen years younger than Gaudí and seventeen years younger than Domènech, straddles the age of *Modernisme* and that of *Noucentisme*. It was perhaps a degree of 'generational' reaction which turned his interest back to the unfinished work of the early Romantics of the *Renaixença*. In a scrupulously scientific way he consummated the process of recovery of the past through his studies of Romanesque architecture: the three volumes of *L'arquitectura romànica a Catalunya* (1908-1918) with Goday and Folguera, and his two-volume *Arquitectura* (1901) within the *Historia general del Arte* edited by Domènech. If we simplistically consider *Modernisme* to be a version of *Art Nouveau*, then Puig, who never used a sinuous wave in his life, would be excluded from the movement. This fact itself underlines how *Modernisme* is to be understood fundamentally in terms of its underlying cultural and 'political' motivation, beyond the diverse (even contradictory) stylistic modes which it generated. What Puig i Cadafalch did do was to join the *Renaixença* nostalgia for an authentic past with the ideals of a modern, European and institutionalized Catalonia projected into the twentieth century, that global *modernista* aspiration which the ensuing movement of *Noucentisme* (emphasizing the break between the old century and the new, the 'nineteen hundreds') would appropriate, refine and endow with specific aesthetic

Antoni Gaudí, Casa Milà, 1905-1911.

Antoni Gaudí, Church of the Sagrada Família, 1884-1926.

and political connotations. In fact, throughout Puig's brief architectural career of fifteen years, we detect the imprint of his original *modernista* affiliation and, in particular, the influence of his teacher, Domènech. The red brick with stone dressing, the careful location of exuberant floral motifs in sculptural decoration, the glazed tilework and coloured glass, all identify him with the local architecture of his time. It is significant that his *Casa Martí* (1896) should have housed Pere Romeu's famous *Quatre Gats* café (from 1897 to 1903) which, following on from Santiago Rusiñol's *Festes modernistes* of the 1890s, was the centre of *Modernisme's* bohemia and the hotbed of the movement's militant artistic spirit. Through his studies and his travels, Puig was more in touch with European culture than either Domènech or Gaudí. If he was not so important a renovator in architecture it was perhaps because of the combined effects of the breadth of his cultural interests and of his political activities. What he did bring to *Modernisme* was the historical depth of a sound (even classic) understanding of medieval architecture united to the physicist-mathematician's scientific acceptance of the machine age. He was, moreover, the chief proponent of the Arts and Crafts movement in Catalonia, the source of that domestic fragrance which permeates all his architecture. It is felt, first and foremost, in his own house in Argentona (1897-1900), a conversion of three village dwellings into a picturesque continuity of internal spaces, and then in nearly a dozen private houses, in the city and in the country, including such notable buidings as the *Casa Garí* (1900) and the *Casa Amatller* (1898-1900). When, as in the latter houses and in the *Casa Macaya* (1901), Puig was working on a large scale, he sought deliberately to evoke the medieval noble and merchant palaces, like those in the carrer Montcada, with their central entrance courtyards and open staircases rising up to the first floor.

Alexandre Cirici divided Puig's work into three phases: the pink or nostalgic (brick), the white or civilized (stucco with classical *sgraffito*, exposed stone frames around doors and windows), and the yellow or plutocratic (monumental classic). The classification is helpful as long as we appreciate that the distinctions are not chronological. There is in Puig a hesitation between local historical resources, current fashions generated by the Austrian Secession and his search for an appropriate Mediterranean medium. While his styling might be eclectic, however, the central consistency of his architecture is in the strong personal stamp which he gave to his individual synthesis of apparently opposing cultural tendencies: medieval and Baroque, local and European, artisan and technological. He was closer to the spirit of William Morris than any of his compatriots, and as a consequence came close to the English Free Architecture of the turn of the century in a parallel attempt to establish a Catalan equivalent.

Puig's international associations do not stop here. It was a very young Walter Gropius who left Berlin in 1903 (according to some it was 1906) and travelled to Spain 'to immerse himself in another culture in order to find himself' (conversation with the author, Barcelona 1969). Gropius, sixteen years younger than Puig, was absorbed by what the Catalan explained to him about workshop production and about craftsmen engaged in what we today call industrial design (probably referring to the influential workshop of Domènech and Gallissà). On his last visit to Barcelona, shortly before his death in 1969, the father of twentieth-century architecture recalled how his encounter with Puig had been influential in his founding of the famous Bauhaus school of design in 1919. We have, then, a direct intellectual link between *Modernisme* and the Rationalist architecture of Europe in the 1920's, *via* the German *Verkbund* which was founded in 1907 to bridge the gulf between art and industry. Many similarities emerge between Puig's position in Catalonia and that of the fathers of the *Deutsche Werkbund*, who, as Joan Campbell expresses it, were ambivalent in their 'romantic nostalgia for a lost world combined with determination to meet contemporary needs', affected as they were by a purpose which was 'essentially a conservative one, namely to restore the lost moral and aesthetic unity of German culture'. This perspective on *Modernisme* as a whole is a most illuminating one.

Puig himself was intensely conscious of participating in an architectural movement of great cultural and historical significance. In the introduction to a book on his own work, *L'œuvre de Puig Cadafalch architecte 1896-1904*, published on the occasion of the 1904 Architects' Congress in Madrid, he surveyed the current state of Catalan architecture. The nineteenth-century panorama is envisaged thus: after over half a century of relying on poor and crude copies from France, Barcelona became a rich and lively centre with a desire to build a large city and the need to acquire quickly an art that had to be created, shaped and improvised. A real sense of urgency and exhilaration is conveyed in the description of contemporary achievements in filling this void: 'It was like this: in a moment the teaching of architecture was improvised, even more quickly teachers and pupils were formed, and schools were set up, each one going its own way; some searched for an impossible restoration of a new Romanesque art; some imported the neo-gothic French school of Viollet-le-Duc, or searched for the new art in Germany, Austria, France; some practiced a rational architecture exposing the material and structure. From all this probably the most positive thing is that between all of us we have produced a modern art, based on our own traditional art, ornamenting it with the beauty of new materials using a rational spirit to solve today's problems, grafting on to it exuberant medieval decorations

Antoni Gaudí, Güell Park, 1904-1914.

and even a certain overlay of semi-Moorish and vague visions from the Far East. It has been a collective work of unconscious visionaries...' The author's own words and practice would contradict this last idea (in which we detect, incidentally, the origins of a distorting myth about *Modernisme* which the *noucentistes* would exploit to the full), as would the conclusion in which Puig identifies his work with that of other young architects eager to create a 'new art characteristic of our times'. It was a collective enterprise that, with attention fixed on developments abroad (especially through publications), understood how there was a new architecture, universal in spirit but rooted in the character of each country and community.

Puig i Cadafalch's finest building, and the one which most fully embodies the principles expressed in his writing, is undoubtedly the *Casa Terrades* popularly known as the *Casa de les Punxes* (1903-1905). It occupies a triangular site between the Avinguda Diagonal and the carrer Rosselló, one of Cerdà's awkward sliced islands that lie along the broad diagonal intersection. The large, medieval-inspired apartment building, topped with steep gabled roofs that are almost Dutch-looking, is articulated at each corner with a cylindrical tower and steeple. What is beautifully handled is the way that these gabled facades overlap the towers without actually touching them. The towers themselves, through their circular plan, turn each corner effortlessly so that the building never loses its unity, while at the same time its domestic quality is affirmed through the breaking up of its volumes and the small scale of its windows.

National politics merged with Puig's architectural profession, ultimately to predominate. He was elected to the Municipal Council in 1901 for Dr. Robert's conservative nationalist party, the *Lliga Regionalista*. In charge of public works, Puig set up a museums committee, initiated building of a new drainage system and organized

Antoni Gaudí, Bellesguard, 1900-1910.

Antoni Gaudí, Bellesguard, 1900-1910.

a competition for altering Cerdà's plan to improve communications with the surrounding townships absorbed into the growing metropolis. The competition was won by the Frenchman Léon Jaussely with a project that the jury found 'most beautiful ... most monumental'. It is an indication of the critical attitude towards Cerdà's plan that was gaining ground, associated with the desire to introduce a hierarchical system more acceptable to the conservative ruling class whose sway in local politics was now overwhelming. Puig's political career eventually took him to the Presidency of the *Mancomunitat*, between 1917 and 1924, where he headed the semi-devolved government of the united provinces of the Principality of Catalonia which had been established under Prat de la Riba's leadership of the *Lliga Regionalista*. With the *coup d'état* of General Primo de Rivera, heralding the end of the *Mancomunitat*, Puig retired to pursue his studies, academic life and lecturing abroad.

The intertwining stories of these three architects — Lluís Domènech, Antoni Gaudí and Josep Puig i Cadafalch — represent the most brilliant illustration of the modern Romantics in their search for and affirmation of identity in the present. Three men embarked on the same route, tackling the same problems, each one concerned with a reinterpretation of tradition, the use of new materials and the creation of form from new necessities, each one variously integrating Nature into the design and decoration of buildings, but each, ultimately, expressing himself in a quite distinctive way. Domènech, rational with eclectic decoration; Gaudí caught up with a total idea that flows through and gives a Baroque shape to the whole; Puig, patriotic and European, adroitly steering between the medieval and the classic. All three lived intensely the vitality of their own present, sensitively and skilfully expressed in their work. Posterity is fortunate to have a joint monument to them, and to *modernista* archi-

Antoni Gaudí, Güell Gatehouse and Stables, 1887.

Antoni Gaudí, Güell Park, 1904-1914.

tecture, in the popularly named *Mansana de la discòrdia*, Gaudí's *Casa Batlló* flanked by Puig's *Casa Amatller* and Domènech's *Casa Lleó Morera*, majestically dominating the Passeig de Gràcia, harmonious in their 'dissonance'.

It would be wrong, however, to limit illustration of *Modernisme* in architecture to the work of these three towering figures. To do so would be to distort an essential characteristic of the movement, the way in which it educated public taste, gave widespread circulation to the new stylistic possibilities, cultivating them as a sort of architectural vernacular remarkable for its quantity as well as its quality. In this, indeed, *Modernisme* differed from the more exclusive acceptance elsewhere of *Art Nouveau* and of the (expensive) products of the Arts and Crafts movement, however much basic inspiration it derived from them. Thus the use of designs and motifs taken from Nature had an important role in popularizing *modernista* fashion, uniting a certain pragmatic realism with a sentimental reaction against industrial squalor that the middle classes as a whole could easily identify with. Furthermore, *Modernisme*, while asserting a modern, cosmopolitan image, was able to reconcile this, in theory and in practice, with the revaluation of individual craftsmanship and local traditions, both of which were still strongly present in the late nineteenth-century Catalan context. To these favourable conditions should be added the élan and confidence of the movement that proclaimed the value of inspiration and the freedom of the spirit. In the particular domain of architecture these impulses meant, above all, a break away from rigid academic classicism and a positive emphasis upon creative participation. Architects, craftsmen and clients came together as a team, conscious in varying degrees of the spirit of the age, tradition and progress charged with a rising current of nationalism. This unique combination of conditions explains the plethora of 'vernacu-

Antoni Gaudí, Church of the Colònia Güell, 1898-1915.

Antoni Gaudí, the square in Güell Park, 1904-1914 (drawing by Elies Torres and Martínez Lapeña)

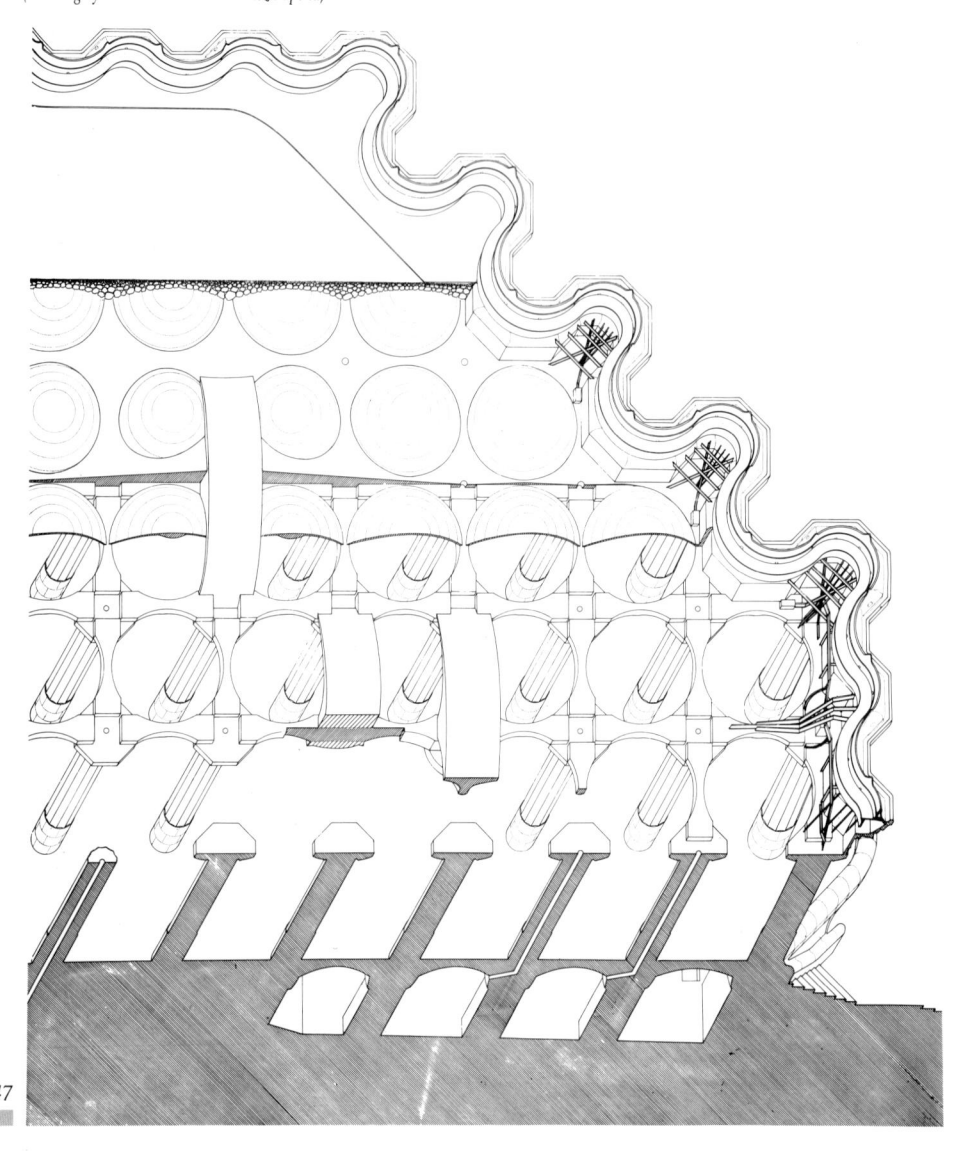

lar' *Modernisme*, the background to its masterpieces, in the hundreds of private and public buildings which make Catalonia and its capital one of the richest concentrations of *fin de siècle* architectural creativity in the world. The artistic movement, as we have stressed, cannot be detached from its socio-political context, and the same is true of its eventual decline. *Modernisme* was born out of a revolt againts the established academicism and was shot through with an idealism whose ideological implications were of a progressive liberal, socialist or even, at certain extremes, anarchist slant. In the turbulence of political realignments of the new century, the upper-middle classes now dominating nationalism and definitively installed as the local power block, came to suspect *Modernisme*'s dissolvent tendencies and to repudiate its artistic language: the process culminated in *Noucentisme*. There was a *modernista* reaction which took the form of an extreme romantic naturalism of floridness, with anarchic connotation (aspects of the *Parc Güell* and Jujol's *Can Negre* at Sant Joan Despí, as prime examples), and this in itself blocked off the possibility of a rational simplification of the movement. The ideals were weakened (or transferred to the *noucentista* ranks), the clientele shifted and, towards the later years, the vernacular *modernista* styles degenerated into hackneyed and stereotyped mimicry. Progressivism thus denatured reverted to being another sterile academicism.

There are other problems of historical focus and interpretation of *Modernisme*. The age of the modern romantics merges to such an extent with the *Renaixença* precursors on one side and with the backlash of *Noucentisme* on the other that *Modernisme* can be subjected to a kind of pincer-movement of reductionism, confining it to the explosion of the odd handful of brilliant buildings by the leading figures. An adjustment of the optic, on the other hand, produces the opposing vision and response by which the histori-

Antoni Gaudí, Colònia Güell, plan of the church, 1898-1915.

an, confronted by the sheer abundance of production with its variable eclectic manners, gradations and overlaps of styles and *œuvres*, has wanted to bundle everything together and give it a single label, so that *Modernisme* is made to spread both ways to include the early romantics of the *Renaixença* and the ideal romantics of *Noucentisme*. For the clarity of our own picture, it will be helpful, then, to complete our conspectus of *Modernisme* in a measured chronology which will take us from the Exhibition of 1888 through to 1914 and the very first years of the *Mancomunitat*.

Just as Gaudí finished his *Palau Güell* (an account of which was published in Boston in the *American Architect and Building News*, July 1892, after an American deputation had come over to celebrate the Columbus monument inaugurated during the Exhibition), Francesc Berenguer (1866-1914) finished his warehouse or winecellar at Garraf, also for Güell. The two architects were lifelong intimate friends and collaborators. Their strong personalities complemented each other: Gaudí emotional, idealistic and a fervent conversationalist; Berenguer, quiet, a careful organizer and indefatigable worker. Both came from the small market-town of Reus where they had attended the school run by Berenguer's father. Berenguer never finished his architectural studies, having married early, and he was employed as assistant to several architects including Gaudí whose name was officially put to several of the former's projects. The Garraf winestore (1888-1890) is a triangular prism with leaning walls, in which there is no distinction between wall and roof and which appears as one continuous stony volume. Several commentators have pointed out that there is a certain resemblance between this work and Gaudí's *Bellesguard*, in whose execution Berenguer intervened directly. The latter had also done numerous drawings for the façade of the *Palau Güell*, and there is a visible similarity between the stone mullions used in the gallery of the palace and in the *Bodega* porch. This geometrical schematization of cubist forms, exploiting variations on the cylinder, cube and prism, is seen in much of Berenguer's work, perhaps most notably in the interior elevation of the Nativity facade of the *Sagrada Família* which he worked on for most of his life. Basically, we can detect in this simplification of form echoes of the neo-Romanesque *Rundbogenstil*, with the important elimination of the arch. Bur there is now a strong overlay of pictorial influence, specifically that of the Impressionists and the discipline of Cézanne, with the subjection of the parts to a multiple disintegration of the whole. Translated into architecture, these principles encouraged the tendency for the individual building to be conceived as an integrated artistic whole, where the dominant impact is that of the creative architectural *impression*. In practice, this theory converged quite naturally with that of *erstarrte Musik* which was, as we have seen, a major influence in expanding the architectural vocabulary of *Modernisme*. The Garraf building is in many ways a textbook exemplar of these currents. What we see is, in essence, just a stone roof over the wine vats, the germ of the architectural *impression* which owes its simplicity to the early huts explained by Vitruvius, the Roman architect who would have figured prominently on the syllabus organized by E. Rogent at the Barcelona school of architecture. Once again we are made aware of how the search for authentic origins is integrated with innovation in the architecture of *Modernisme*.

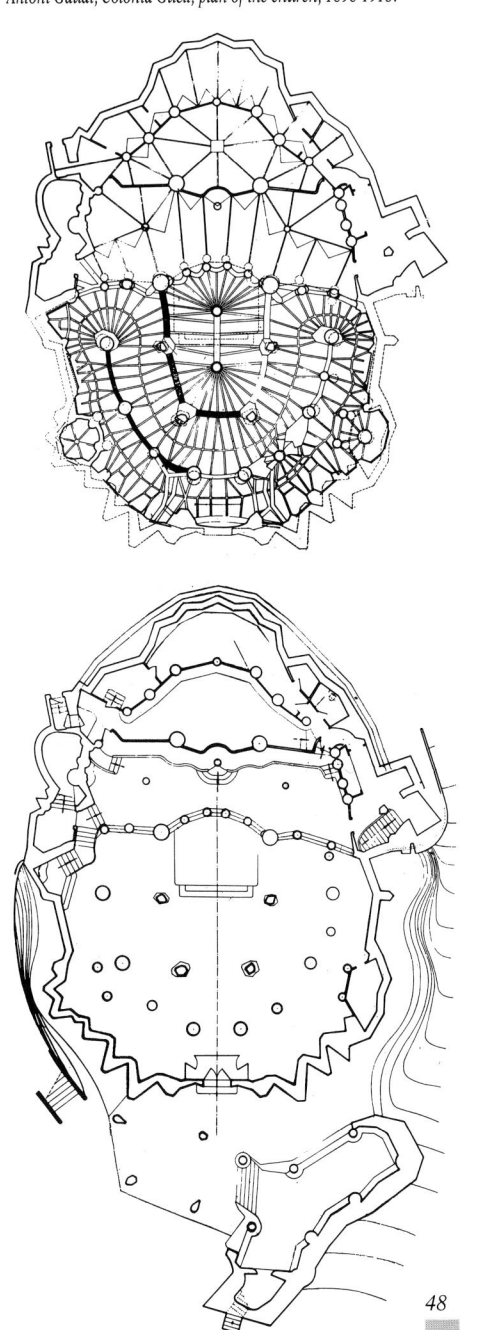

A little further down the Garraf coast, Francesc Rogent was adapting a set of houses perched on the cliffs above the breaking waves of the Mediterranean at Sitges, commissioned by the writer and painter Santiago Rusiñol. The *Cau Ferrat* was to house not only the artist's collection of antique ironwork but also the setting for his *Festes modernistes*, from 1892 to 1899, the

Pablo Picasso, 4 Gats menu, 1899-1900.

early focal point of *Modernisme's* artistic challenge to a materialistic and 'soulless' society. The building survives as a symbol of the modernist spirit in Catalonia and of the fertile artistic syncretism through which it operated.

There were, of course, distractions from the cause in the direction of 'pure' politics (witness Domènech's consuming involvement in the *Bases de Manresa*). And there was also opposition, notably that which centred on the influential Bishop of Vic, Torres i Bages, whose book *La tradició catalana* inspired the artistic conservatism of the *Cercle Artístic de Sant Lluc*. But Barcelona was meanwhile giving an increasingly enthusiastic welcome to the modern trends offered by European culture. Wagner's *Tannhäuser* was performed at the Liceu, majestically consolidating the spirit of the new Romanticism and offering a sort of reassurance of social stability. Berenguer built one of the last iron markets, the *Mercat de la Llibertat* (1893) in Gràcia, with swirling *Art Nouveau* decoration. The following year saw completion of Gaudí's convent for the Teresians, described above. Industrial expansion showed a symbolic front in Josep Domènech i Estapà's headquarters for the *Catalana de Gas i Electricitat* (1895), crowning the process that had begun with the introduction of gas streetlighting in 1842. The building is marked by the author's monumental tendencies, both in the entrance sequence and the formal composition of the façade whose rather tired eclectic elements are borrowed from his earlier Palace of Justice, begun in 1887 in collaboration with Enric Sagnier.

Puig i Cadafalch built his 'medieval' *Casa Martí* where, in the shape of the famous *Quatre Gats* café, the spirit of Rusiñol's *Festes modernistes* was installed in the very heart of the capital. Despite the wars in Morocco and in Cuba, and despite the ominous anarchist outrages which began with the bomb at the Liceu in 1892, a breath of freedom and fresh air was blowing

Josep Puig i Cadafalch, Casa Puig, 1897-1900.

Josep Puig i Cadafalch, Casa Quadras, 1904.

Josep Puig i Cadafalch, Casa Amatller, 1898-1900.

through the social life of bourgeois Barcelona. Sport and the open air became symbols of the breaking down of inhibitions and made a clear imprint in fashion. The functionalism of the bicycle sums up much of the mood of freedom and novelty. It is an image which unites Ramon Casas's massive mural (the artist and Pere Romeu riding a carefree tandem) from the *Quatre Gats* and Puig's cycle journeys across Barcelona to supervise building of the *Casa Macaya*, where a bicycle is playfully illustrated in one of the 'medieval' corbels by the door.

The loss of the colonies, Cuba, Puerto Rico and the Phillipines, appeared to have no negative effect on the boom in production of fine buildings over the turn of the century. Architecture, or rather the building industry, has its own momentum and particular cycles of prosperity, and the buoyancy of the new century carried through the immense building work of the expanding city for at least a decade. The year of political crisis, 1898, saw the installation of the first mechanical lift in Barcelona. It was the moment of the great private houses: Domènech's *Casa Thomas* and Puig's *Casa Garí* were followed by the latter's own house in Argentona, then the *Casa Amatller* and the Macaya and Muntades houses; then came Domènech's *Casa Navàs* in Reus, Joan Rubió's (1871-1952) Alemany, Frare Blanc and Golferichs houses, using rubble stone with brick edgings, and Gaudí's imposing *Bellesguard*. One notes in these and other examples a certain 'family resemblance' —a function of fashion in the context of a social class asserting its new wealth and national identity— together with evidence of each client's (and his architect's) urge to affirm his individuality. The rich choice of architects available allowed the bourgeoisie to indulge in this 'conspicuous consumption', legitimated both by individualism and by patriotism.

It was, however, inevitable that the gathering social tensions which were already being felt

Josep Puig i Cadafalch, Casa Macaya, 1901.

would break dramatically into the foreground. The political consequences of the new orientation taken by Catalan nationalism in the early twentieth century would have pronounced reverberations in the cultural sphere, throwing into crisis the apparently unified momentum of *Modernisme*. As though anticipating this, *modernista* artists had already intuited and expressed underlying strains of a divided society, as in some canvases of Casas, many by Nonell and the early Picasso, and in the 'black' writing of visionaries including the young Eugeni d'Ors. With key magazines like *Quatre Gats* and *Pèl & Ploma* already defunct, the important journal *Joventut* represented the swan-song of what might be termed cultural nationalism in its *modernista* version. Signs of a conservative reaction were strongly in the air, emanating from politics but affecting all aspects of cultural activity. As regards architecture, there is much that is symptomatic in the two articles published by the young architect Jeroni Martorell (1877-1951) in the magazine *Catalunya* on the subject of the Secession movement in Vienna. The movement, dating from 1897, stood for a break with the Academy and a trend, led by the architect Otto Wagner, to cultivate surface decoration clinging to formal classical compositions: the literary magazine *Catalunya*, edited by the up-and-coming poet Josep Carner, while ostensibly independent in outlook, contained in embryo the spirit and the cultural programmes of *Noucentisme*.

1904 is full of indications of transition. While Domènech i Estapà was building his *Hospital Clínic*, the new prison and the Fabra Observatory in his stark, heavy-handed and sexless style of stripped classical convention, Puig described a delicately rococo, central European-type domestic architecture in his *Casa Trinxet* or overlaid floral and Gothic motifs in his *Casa Quadres*, and Domènech i Montaner began the final flourish of *Modernisme* in the *Palau de la Música Catalana*. The controversial visit to Barcelona of the new

Josep Puig i Cadafalch, Casa Macaya, Patio, 1901.

king Alfonso XIII exposed one set of divisions among the Catalans. Another set is dramatically summed up in Ramon Casas's painting *La càrrega*, with its immense, empty white space between the mounted Civil Guards and the demonstrators. The glaring space of social inequality and injustice, the class conflict which the euphoria of modernization had temporarily masked but which, after rapid social expansion without institutional checks on abuse, was bound to erupt into the historical foreground. All the other manifestations of division and transition were, ultimately, subject to this reality.

In 1905 Domènech's Lleó Morera house in the Passeig de Gràcia was completed, Vilaseca finished his richly ornamented house for Cabot, and Puig the superbly articulated *Casa de les Punxes*. The real shift in cultural ideology and authority, however, was continuing apace. The last issue of the journal *La Renaixença* virtually coincided with the rise to prominence of the young critic *Xènius*, Eugeni d'Ors, who from 1906 onwards preached a more classical, Mediterranean version of national identity and cultural discipline. The *Glosari*, as his epigrammatic pronouncements were entitled, occupied the front page of the daily *La Veu de Catalunya*, the organ of the *Lliga Regionalista*.

Architecture was inevitably a focal point for some of these developments. Francesc Galí, who had abandoned his architectural studies to study painting and drawing, set up his own school of art in 1906. Its guiding principles were humanistic and, coinciding with the classicism propounded by *Xènius*, the questing look for inspiration was turned away from the Central and Northern European cultures, towards the Mediterranean and, in particular, the Italy that Ruskin had exalted. Even so, the changing theory of 1906 still did not cut off the full flowering of *modernista* building. Gaudí confidently finished his contribution, the *Casa Batlló*, to that impressive threesome in the Passeig de Gràcia, and the younger generation built houses outside Barcelona, like Manuel Raspall (1877-1937) in La Garriga, Eduard Balcells (1877-1965) in Sant Cugat and Cerdanyola, Pau Monguió (1865-1956) in Teruel, and Rafael Masó (1881-1935) in Girona. Lluís Muncunill (1868-1931) applied his knowledge of the Catalan vault, so well exploited by Gaudí in the crypt of the *Colonia Güell* and in the parish school of the *Sagrada Família*, to Catalan industry. His Aymerich i Amat factory (1907) with its extensive shell vaults is both assertively modern-looking, echoing the expressionist waves of the recently formed *Die Brücke* group at Dresden (1905), and at the same time well anchored in the local brick tradition, touched with a simplified eclectic vocabulary deriving from the first-generation modernists. His *Masia Freixa*, also of 1907, now the municipal school of music, is an eye-catching construction but one which, from our perspective, is eccentric to Muncunill's major works. There is a capriciousness about the vigorous and strange expressionism of the whole —parabolic arched porches, domed roofs and mannered tower— that, betrayed in the complete lack of attention to detail, makes this a crude and curiously disappointing building.

Lluís Domènech did not attend the opening of the *Palau de la Música Catalana* in February 1908. We do not know why. Oral history even relates that he never set foot in the building again. We can only guess that, in this crucial period, the architect was afflicted by a crisis in which personal, political and artistic factors were all combined. Joaquim Cabot, rich businessman, *Lliga* politican and president of the *Orfeó Català* choir, in his inaugural address, was unstinting in his praise of Domènech's inseparable artistic genius and great patriotism. In the background, though, there were serious rifts in the *Solidaritat Catalana* movement, a shot-gun marriage of pragmatic right and nationalist left parties (the latter represented by Domènech) which failed in the 1908 elections to stem the tide of Lerroux's demagogic and anti-Catalanist republicanism. The collapse of *Solidaritat Catalana* was a crucial stage in the discrediting of values associated with *Modernisme*.

Another palace was completed in 1908, the Palace of Justice by J. Domènech i Estapà and Enric Sagnier. Begun in 1887, its construction covers almost the complete period of *Modernisme*, to whose ideals and artistic experiments it offers a kind of heavy counterpoint. In a historical sense we can see this building as bridging together *Reinaxença* neoclassic with the new classicism of the institution-minded proponents of an Ideal Catalonia: the ethics and aesthetics of *Noucentisme* preached by Eugeni d'Ors, in the service of the *Lliga's* political programme, now headed by Enric Prat de la Riba from the Presidency of the Diputació de Barcelona (county council), the first step towards the formation of the *Mancomunitat*.

The circumstances, the outburst of pent-up violence and the eventual reprisals of the Tragic Week in Barcelona (from July 26, 1909) had the effect of further increasing the conservative classes' isolation from popular grievances and of increasing their reliance on the 'civilizing order' proposed by the *Lliga*. It was in this year that Gaudí built his little parish school to the side of the *Sagrada Família*. Now nearly sixty, the architect was himself becoming isolated from society. His last major civil works —the *Parc Güell*, the *Casa Milà*— were in the final stages of completion and he was becoming more and more enclosed in the religious world of his great temple. Thus safely cut off and innocuous, society could now honour him, which it did through Güell himself who arranged for an exhibition of his work in the architectural section of the *Société Nationale des Beaux Arts* in 1910, supervised by Jeroni Martorell. There is a certain irony in the fact that it was the same year in which the American Frank Lloyd Wright's

*Josep Puig i Cadafalch, Casa Terradas
(Casa de les Punxes – House of Spires) 1903-1905.*

Francesc Berenguer, Wine-cellar, Dwellings and Chapel, Garraf, 1888-1890.

Francesc Berenguer, Liberty Market, 1893.

work, in an exhibition in Berlin, was first displayed to the world.

Lluís Domènech completed his *Casa Fuster* at the top of the Passeig de Gràcia and also the first stage of the *Hospital Sant Pau*. A year later Puig finished his large *Casarramona* brick factory in Montjuïc. The year 1911 was a major cultural watershed: the death of the poet Maragall seemed to signal, in Enric Jardí's words, '*Modernisme's* liquidation and *Noucentisme's* coming of age'. The last was confirmed by the publication (1912) of Eugeni d'Ors's *La Ben Plantada*, a strangely disembodied symbolic fiction whose true significance was well described by Miguel de Unamuno when he called it a 'concise aesthetico-political gospel': the aesthetics of *Noucentisme*, that is, inseparable from the politics of the *Lliga*. From his position as secretary of the newly founded *Institut d'Estudis Catalans*, Ors gave momentum to the new mobilization of Catalan intellectuals in the 'civilizing ideal' and the institutionalization (reform 'from above') of Catalan culture. The anti-*modernista* ideology thus achieved institutional status. Even Domènech i Estapà read a paper to the Academy of Sciences attacking *Modernisme*. But what was left of the movement as a dynamic force was already changing. The influence of the Viennese Secession was strongly apparent. Josep M. Pericas (1881-1966), who designed the monument to the poet Verdaguer in 1913 (built 1924), had already designed and was constructing his parish church of the Carme (1910-1914), brick-built with soft round corners and articulated façade elements that remind one of the architecture of Amsterdam. His *Casa Comella* (1912) followed the chromatic designs of Puig but played with the volumes in a picturesque way that is obviously related to the domestic buildings of the Darmstadt exhibition of 1901. The final (and divergent) ramifications of this trend are to be seen in the later works of Masó (houses and hotel at S'Agaró, 1929-35) and Jujol (from the *Torre de la*

Josep Puig i Cadafalch, Casarramona Yarn Factory, 1911.

Creu, 1913, to his houses in Sant Joan Despí, *Casa Serra*, 1927, and *Casa Jujol*, 1932).

The Modern Romantics were unable to complete their task of assimilating the Early Romantics' recovery of the past to the energies and the realities of the present. Their fervent cult of cosmopolitan modernity, fired by the prevailing aesthetic of creative individualism by which local tradition and universalism were united, gradually coalesced as a concerted movement only at the point where it was recognized as such by its enemies and confronted by a concerted reaction which quickly produced its demoralization. It was the satirical attacks of reviews like *L'Esquella de la Torratxa* or the scathing criticism by Eugeni d'Ors that first clarified and showed the coherence of their works. From our perspective we can now perceive those strong elements of cultural and ideological consistency that drew them together, more stable that the apparent contradictions and the apparent dispersion of aesthetic signs. By the second decade of the twentieth century it had become the task of the younger generation to invert the terms of the preceding explosion of cultural vitality. Culture *per se* was no longer seen as a transcendental force that could open the gates to the political advance of nationalism. Instead the politics of culture were to establish the ideal conditions in which Civilization could exist and prosper.

Lluís Muncunill, Aymerich i Amat Factory (Terrassa), 1907.

Lluís Muncunill, Freixa Farm House converted into factory (Terrassa), 1907.

Rafael Masó, Teixidor Flour Mill Factory (Girona), 1910-1911.

III

THE IDEAL ROMANTICS: A SEARCH FOR INSTITUTIONAL IDENTITY

The rejection of academic classicism, originated by Viollet-le-Duc, Ruskin and Morris, sparked off an almost anarchic search for an art that could be identified with the present and the excitement of modernity. As we have seen: the panhistorical vision produced an electric vocabulary; Viollet-le-Duc's constructional analyses suggested a more scientific approach to the art of building; Ruskin's mountain doctrine inspired an organic relationship between the sublimity of the Gothic landscape and Gothic architecture. These approaches found echo in the sinuous lines of a Catholic *Art Nouveau* on the one hand, and in the disciplined domestic work tradition of the Protestant Arts and Crafts movement on the other.

Catalan culture, always at the cross-roads of European movements, absorbed these tendencies through Gaudí, Domènech and Puig, reshaping their contradictory aspects to produce the finest examples of national Modernist architecture: a Romantic architecture that, while harking back to an idealized medieval era, was free to respond to the functional requirements of a new mode, personally interpreted and popularly understood as being appropriate to the aspirations and self-image of a country that wished to express both its unique personality and its integral modernity. For it was precisely this modernity that set off Catalonia from the rest of Spain, as a socio-economic and 'temperamental' reality that was expressed as a firm gaze upon Europe and a finger upon its cultural pulse. Just as *Modernisme* was reaching its climax with its characteristic synthesis of European strains, many of the premises and cultural values on which the movement was based (outstandingly, Ruskinian 'naturalism') began to be energetically rejected in Europe itself.

This rejection responded to two distinct but related attitudes. One was the emotive, outright repudiation of *Art Nouveau* as expressed by the Arts and Crafts architect Charles Voysey, invoking above all the virtues of simplicity. In 1904 he denounced *Art Nouveau* as 'distinctly unhealthy and revolting... Is it not merely the work of a lot of imitators with nothing but mad eccentricity as a guide; good men, no doubt, misled into thinking that art is a debauch of sensuous feeling, instead of the expression of humane thought and feeling combined?'. It was even more radically rejected by the Viennese architect Adolf Loos in 1908, after his stay in the USA, with his famous statement associating ornament with crime and advocating aesthetic puritanism. The other attitude derived from the necessity of finding the roots of local architecture within the corresponding historical tradition, the serious pursuit of which implied a more academic approach to culture. This was expressed by the German architect Hans Poelzig in 1906, with his concern about the right kind of architecture that 'cannot do without the past in solving the architectural problems of our own day', but which at the same time 'carries the banner of objectivity against traditional structures that have become empty of content and petrified into a scheme.' Poelzig concluded that 'for the time being we must demand only unrelenting objectivity and a solution, in keeping with good taste, of a clearly thought out problem.'

The sobriety of English domestic architecture and the elegance of Charles Rennie Mackintosh found fertile ground in the Viennese Secession, the German Darmstadt Exhibition and the later *Deutscher Werkbund* (1907), and then in the national Romanticism of the Scandinavian countries. In Germany there was intense concern about the country's low artistic reputation, generating an enormous effort for recovery of a place in the modern movement. Reverberations of this questioning and surge of activity were felt throughout Europe.

Gaudí, ever more wrapped up in his own preoccupations, ignored these developments abroad, despite having a patron as well-informed as Güell. Domènech, always a rationalist at heart, responded by affirmation of the essential lines of his work in progress rather than by self-criticism, as can be seen in the *Hospital Sant Pau*. Puig, younger and more intellectual, was openly influenced by these European currents. In his case it was sound professionalism which impressed upon all his varied work a serious and academic approach to both the medieval and the classical traditions.

The most active interpreter and relayer in Catalonia of this movement of retrenchment was, as has been indicated, the oracle of *Noucentisme*, Eugeni d'Ors, the *Xènius* of the *Glosari*. Form the authoritative front page of Prat de la Riba's daily *La Veu de Catalunya* he tellingly promoted the values of 'arbitrariness' in art, the domination of form by civilized, rational man, as opposed to the spontaneity and the 'naturalism' exalted by such modern Romantics as Maragall in poetry and Gaudí in architecture. We have stressed already how the reaction was

Josep Pericas, Verdaguer Monument, 1913-1924.

closely tied to a particular version of nationalist politics, administered from above, whose aims were to be achieved through the consolidation of institutions, be they formal and administrative or the 'natural' ones of language and education. Northern Europe continued to offer a model — in the 'normality' of the bourgeois order of the *belle époque*— now more specific, though, and overlaid with a dominant concept of Mediterranean civilization. For the artists who were brought into this mobilization of the country's *forces vives* (the dynamic 'establishment') it meant subordination of freedom to the civilizing order, as exemplified in the 'aesthetico-political' doctrine of Ors's influential *La Ben Plantada* (1912). Here the ideal woman, Teresa, is presented in detail as a convergence of different 'feminine' characteristics formed in the setting of the Mediterranean coastal villages: the sensitiveness acquired under the bright sunlight, the clarity and solid timelessness of classical culture, the motherhood associations of a doctrine of imperial Catalan nationalism wherein politics and aesthetics are inseparable. Ors here was not writing about architecure, but it is easy to envisage the architectural translation of such ideas and emblems. The artificiality of the myth is now transparent: its influence in galvanizing the energies of *Noucentisme*, however, cannot be underestimated.

The symbols of *Modernisme* were deemed inadequate or even disruptive. What was needed was a new set of symbols to correspond to the clarity and conviction of the turn taken by Catalanism, with its particularized concept of national identity, in the new century. In the political sphere the *Lliga* was able to capitalize on the social dynamism which *Modernisme* had activated but failed to channel. The election successes of 1901 confirmed the solidarity of a nationalist block composed of bourgeois and petty bourgeois sectors, with a strong intellectual leaning, that paradoxically 'conservative revolutionary'

Josep Pericas, Church of El Carme, 1910-1914.

formation so characteristic of *noucentista* Catalanism. As the cause of nationalism advanced, the more impressive its achievements under such a sign, so inevitably the gap between rich and poor widened. Where the *noucentistes* expressed concern about this growing rift, as in the case of Ors himself, the conviction was that it would be healed by the progress of bourgeois interests and through the civilizing effects of the institutional coordination of society and culture. With his new wealth (enhanced by Spanish neutrality in World War I), the Catalan bourgeois needed security in his display of culture in order to be recognized in his dominant social role. *Noucentisme* provided a total programme for this modification of taste and values. In some areas (literature and painting, for instance) the transformation was abrupt and radical. In architecture, because of its complex discipline and the resulting length of its cycles of oscillation, the response to changing values was a more gradual affair. It is in this line, nevertheless, that we detect in the first decade of the 20th century the assimilation in Catalonia of influences from the Vienna Secession, from the Darmstadt colony, from Mackintosh in Glasgow, and, in general, a more disciplined use for classical elements and proportions.

The movement aquired more momentum after the Tragic Week in 1909, when the social question exploded violently, the Catalan bourgeoisie sat back in shock, and law and order, the consequence of Pratian politics as preached by Ors, was put into practice as far as Madrid would allow. This is the background to the channelling of nationalist aspirations and the identity quest into the authority of institutions. The projection of the ideal City was in this sense a flight from reality. But even in the movement from the conflictive reality of the present to the ideal of the future, the underlying Romantic continuity was assured. It was a vision of the future — the City, the new Athens — based on an adjusted vision of

Josep Goday, Pere Vila School, 1920-1930.

contemporary European civilization, the bourgeois order of a Europe that no-one could foresee would soon collapse into a fratricidal war. That crisis would have to be confronted after 1917. Meanwhile, the projection of a collective identity based on the Catalans' traditional self-image of *seny* (discrimination, moderation, pragmatism) and embodied in the institutions of the *Mancomunitat* gathered force. The theoreticians (Ors, the historian and critic Pijoan, the art teacher Francesc Galí) promoted the inspiration of Mediterranean classicism, control and *seny*, a feeling for appropriateness, a strong emphasis upon Normality, a rejection of the rhetorical and a return to the intimate, the cult of the *obra ben feta* or small job well done. All this was not suddenly invented with the advent of the new century. Each element was there among the vital disorder of *Modernisme*. What *Noucentisme* did was to refine particular lines from the preceding phase, and channel them in a highly disciplined way. The process is visible in the production of numerous artists, among them Ors himself, the poet Carner or, very symptomatically, the sculptor Aristides Maillol. From his delicate pictorial experiments of the 1890's where a *modernista*-inspired quasi-orientalism prevailed, he moved to a concentration on sculptural figures (via a hesitant transition involving a refinement of realist procedures, *Cyclist* 1907-8) which express a robust synthesis of Mediterranean classicism. With sculpture which offered a direct visual equivalence of Ors's *Ben Plantada*, he established his reputation at home and projected a new image of Catalan nationalism abroad, with important exhibitions in France and Germany.

Under the sign of *Noucentisme*'s cultivation of institutional identity we perceive three distinct modes of stylistic modification: the Secession, symbolic Mediterraneanism and late or qualified *Modernisme*.

The articles in Catalan published in 1903 by Jeroni Martorell, architect of the Sabadell Savings Bank (1905-1915), were boldly entitled 'Modern Architecture' and gave a sympathetic account of the Viennese Secession movement, stressing the importance of its free chromatic transformation of basically classical models. The fact is that Austria and Germany offered positive examples and leadership to the older *modernista* architects and to the first wave of *noucentistes*. The Barcelona school of architecture still has various volumes on Otto Wagner and his disciple Olbrich which show evident signs of heavy student use in copying and tracing. That the new guiding lines for architecture should have come from this quarter is easy to understand if we consider how much more imitable a style and procedure they offered than did the older generation of Barcelona practitioners. The monumental classical massing and chromatic baroque of Wagner gave a European sanction to a conservative return to this mode within the local context. Wagner's version of the Secession is clearly felt in buildings by A. Soler (1874-1949) (*Casa Heribert Pons*, 1907-1909), Domènech i Estapà (*Casa Cucurella*, 1911), E. Ferrés (1880-1928) (*Casa Ferrer Vidal*, 1916, and the Hotel Ritz), and the Valencian Demetri Ribes (1877-1921) (Valencia railway terminal, 1906-1930). It was, however, the language of Olbrich, being more domestic, that proved rather easier to assimilate stylistically. The first to do so was Puig i Cadafalch, in 1901, with his use of popular baroque and local farmhouse features from his *Casa Muntades*, followed up in the *Casa Trinxet* (1904) and in the more ambiguous *Casa Sastre* in Sarrià (1905) similar to his own private dwelling in Argentona. None of this architecture can be clearly labelled as Ideal Romantic or even less as out and out *noucentista*. What unites these examples is the search for a balanced idiom, a restrained and serious attempt to create a 'familiar' combination of flexible classicism with popular tradition. Certainly one can see that the freedom and exuberance of *modernista* language have been deliberately cut back. It was the emergence of a style which, stopping short of the grand symbolic Mediterraneanism proposed by Ors, began to achieve the air of an official civic architecture appropriate to the new idea of the City and to the institutions created under the *Mancomunitat*. Effectively, though, there are only two major examples of public architecture that declare unambiguous and exclusive affinity with the Viennese Secession: the monument to Verdaguer (1913-1924) by J. M. Pericas (1881-1966) and the Athenea in Girona (1913) by Rafael Masó (1881-1935).

Masó's *Casa Masramon* (Olot, 1913) takes us to the domestic sphere to find the liveliest interpretation of Viennese architecture adapted to a Catalan setting. The compact massing of this three-storey house, with its undulating cornice breaking through the broad eaves, under which the slits of horizontal windows vie with the vertical composition of the other window elements, displays a relaxed and happy mixture of local farmhouse baroque with the severe discipline of the Secession's chromatic concepts and style. The interior continues this easy marriage of cultures, with farmhouse inglenooks —such a favourite device of the Arts and Crafts— a staircase decorated with vertical screens that look like an original Mackintosh, or Hoffman, and other glazed screens reproducing the flow of space found in Loos' domestic interiors, the latter influenced in turn by his contact with the American scene.

Masó's earlier work in Girona had already developed a style close to that of C. R. Mackintosh, as for example in the hall of *El Solar* (1906-1907), the staircase of the *Casa Masó* (1911-1912) and especially in the black and white chequered designs for the bedrooms in the same house, and the Adroher shop (1916). He had also dabbled in what can only be described as a decadent *Modernisme* with his design for the offices and manager's house of the *Farinera Teixidor* flour mills

Josep Maria Jujol, Torre de la Creu House (Sant Joan Despí), 1913-1916.

Josep María Jujol, plan of Torre de la Creu House (Sant Joan Despí), 1913-1916.

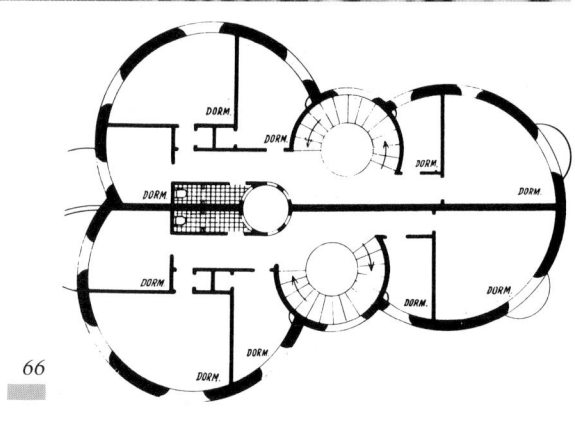

Josep Goday, Baixeras School, 1918-1922.

Josep Goday, plan of the Baixeras School, 1918-1922.

(1910-1911). He continued to mix the horizontal window and tile surfaces with decorations derived from Mackintosh. The roughcast rendering of the plain external walls of both his *Casa Masramon* and *Casa Cendra* (1913-1914) gives way to the fussy and overdrawn work of the Casas house (1915-1916). Where we find a purer Mackintosh style is in the interior of the Ardroher shop (1915-1916). This uncertainty of influences was resolved by the acceptance of the evident contradictions, giving them the stamp of a highly individual manner, as in the *Casa Teixidor* (1918-1922) and *Casa Gispert* (1921-1923). Subsequently he drifted into an established classic rural revivalism at S'Agaró, the Catalan equivalent, in 'comfortableness', of British stockbrokers' Tudor. Tiled roofs, white walls, exposed stone quoins, strings of semi-circular arches, an occasional tower, the stone base, these were the elements of his final vocabulary, so many manifestations of which are to be found throughout Catalonia in the vacation homes of city folk. It was the meeting of two streams of architecture in decadence, derivations of the Secession and a symbolic Mediterraneanism emptied of its cultural contents.

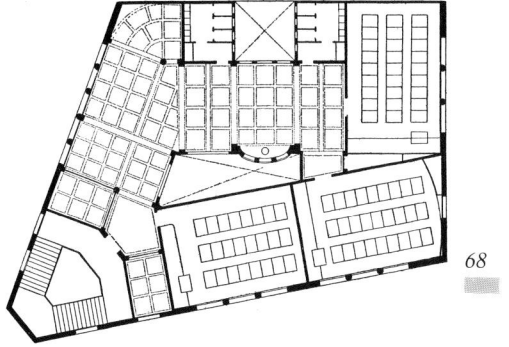

The fact is that this projected symbolic Mediterraneanism, *Noucentisme's* purest architectural equivalence, would have produced virtually nothing in the way of actual constructions completed in its image, were it not, as Oriol Bohigas affirms, for the school buildings of Josep Goday (1882-1936), who worked for Barcelona municipal council from 1916 onwards. A disciple of Puig i Cadafalch, Goday followed the academic discipline of his teacher, putting it into practice in designing for the City Council a series of regular and efficient school buildings in which the planning responded to a progressive educational programme, and in which the role of an aesthetically controlled environment was to play a key part. It was under these governing principles that between 1917 and 1923 the schools named after Baixeras, Lluís Vives, Pere Vila, Ramon Llull and Milà i Fontanals were built.

The story of progressive education in Catalonia is a fascinating one, and one which in many ways runs parallel to the history of its modern architecture. In Spain as a whole, certain liberalizing influences from 19th-century advances in educational theory found their way into the *Ley Moyano* of 1857, a dilute liberal reform law on education which was in practice virtually ineffectual. This law did, however, allow municipal councils to be responsible for putting up schools. In fact, lack of funds prevented any significant municipal initiative, even in Catalonia, until 1914, which saw the creation of the open-air *Escoles Municipals del Bosc* in Montjuïc, followed in 1915 by 15 Montessori schools and in 1916 by plans for the buildings of as many as 37 new schools. Paradoxically there had been, meanwhile, more rapid progress in the private sector, centred on Ferrer i Guàrdia's idea of the *Escola Moderna*, propagating lay and rationalist education among working-class children, which dated from 1901. Five years later there were 47 *Escoles Modernes* in Catalonia. In 1905 Pau Vila founded his *Escola Horaciana*, followed in 1912 by *Mont d'Or* and Alexandre Galí's *Escola Vallparadís*. Thereafter, though, the momentum was transferred to the official sector and to the programme of new schools directed by Goday, from 1917 to 1923.

The quality and distribution of space were immediately appreciated as fundamental factors in the educational process. Goday's official report of 1917 laid emphasis on the quality of the school building itself as contributing to the 'moral formation of the pupils... the spirit of the future citizens of Barcelona, within an evironment of good taste and pleasure'. Moreover, he attached great importance to the idea of 'social education' (in which music and play had major roles), advocating the provision of ample central hall space against the rigid regime of separate classrooms. From the very beginnings of this municipal programme of school-building, then, the concept of the classroom school was being questioned, with positive alternative solutions being proffered. Indeed, the principal effect of Goday's designs was the elimination of the corridor and the grouping of classrooms around the all-important community space.

Of the basic architectural style one can say that it was 'conventional', in that it followed certain rational rules and norms governing composition, structure, disposition of the fenestration and limits of the decoration. This 'normality', though, can in itself be seen to carry an important 'semiotic' charge. The total design is configured by a particular community image (the *noucentista* emphasis on citizenship, civic values and the ideal City echoes in Goday's words quoted above) and by its cultural connotations, at the heart of the administrative undertaking. A classic or classical vocabulary was called for to correspond to the dominant insistence on the Mediterranean essences of Catalan civilization. And, as we have seen, the school building was conceived not merely as a symbol but as a 'social' incarnation of the cultural ideal. It was the strength of such convictions that helped Goday to avoid the trap of historicism into which he might easily have fallen (as he was so accused by the rationalist GATCPAC architects in the 1930's). The decoration, with terracotta and *esgrafiats* by Francesc Canyelles, was based on classical motifs, but both the distribution in plan and the simple window composition of the facades display a conscious effort to adjust and adapt classical rules to a rational interpretation of the brief.

It is worth concentrating for a moment on the most revolutionary design, and brief, of the whole programme of buildings. The *Escola del Mar* (1921), a two-storey, U-shaped timber building on concrete pillars, set lengthways along the shore-line of Barceloneta, was de-

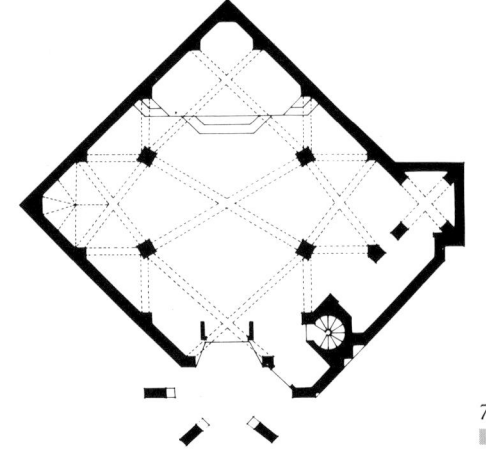

Josep Maria Jujol, Vistabella Church (Tarragona), 1918-1923.

Josep Maria Jujol, plan of Vistabella Church (Tarragona), 1918-1923.

Josep Maria Jujol, Vistabella Church (Tarragona), 1918-1923.

Josep Maria Jujol, Casa Bofarull (Els Pallaresos), 1914-1931.

signed to house not only the usual school but also summer colonies during vacations. Insofar as it was to accommodate the normal school functions, the plan preserved the basic scheme of the other schools: the central hall for community activities, with classrooms on either side. On the other hand, insofar as its use extended beyond the normal limits of a school brief, the U-shape at one and the same time adapted the building to its particular urban context (Barceloneta's 45° street layout) and embraced a stretch of beach for recreational purposes as well as for outdoor teaching. We can observe here how, by adopting a conventional architectural style, the architect was able to concentrate on those essential and specific (and distinctly modern) features of the plan corresponding to a progressive educational programme. The style, if anything, helped to organize basic conceptions into rational and easily understood containers. Likewise, baroque layout and aggregated decoration are here used expressively to impose a civic and institutional character.

This institutional character was of course fundamental to the image of an Ideal Catalonia deep at the heart of the bourgeois Catalanism presided over by Prat de la Riba. On the occasion of Prat's death in 1917, Folch i Torres declared that 'Art was for him the style of the nation'. The formula, with its specialized conceptions of both 'Art' and 'Nation', summarizes the dynamics of *Noucentisme's* cultural politics, and points as well to its inevitable limitations. 1917 was indeed a crucial year for Catalonia, the beginning of a period of social unrest which the artificial wealth created by the European war could not disguise. Prices soared; strikes and violent labour conflicts proliferated; the Catalan republican and proletarian parties presented an increasingly united and vocal opposition to the now entrenched conservative establishment; a succession of Spanish governments failed to contain instability and confusion; the military, or-

Josep Maria Jujol, Casa Bofarull (Els Pallaresos), 1914-1931.

Josep Maria Jujol, Casa Negre (Sant Joan Despí), 1914-1930.

ganizing its own *Juntas de Defensa*, operated an ominous pressure on civilian politics; the monarchy itself was discredited by the army's ignominious defeat in Morocco in 1921. Liberal attempts to weaken the hold of the oligarchy and to democratize parliamentary power were, in Raymond Carr's words, 'strangled at birth' when, supported by the King and by the most conservative sectors of a nervous Catalan bourgeoisie, General Primo de Rivera's coup was effected in September 1923.

Within this unsettling political and social context, Catalanism, enacted as the Ideal Romantics' search for institutional identity, became more urgent as it became more embattled and fragile. Just as the *modernistes*, over the turn of the century, flourished most effusively as the seeds of the 'idealist' reaction were already being cast, so the high point of artistic *Noucentisme* also coincided with signs of crisis and internal division. The Dadaism of Francis Picabia, new contacts with the European vanguard centred on Josep Dalmau's famous gallery, the about-turn of the painter and critic Joaquim Torres Garcia, the sort of iconoclasm espoused in the early writings of the poet Salvat-Papasseit, all indicated a reaction against the orderly mobilization of cultural efforts in the service of a political ideal, a reaction expressed as reaffirmation of the autonomy of individual inspiration and creation. The cultural ferment did not gather into a single, coherent philosophy, and in this sense it can be seen to mirror the absence of concerted solutions to pressing social and political questions. Certainly, though, we can locate in this period the beginnings of a serious break with the Romantic fervour which in various guises, had sustained cultural Catalanism since its 19th-century beginnings. What was prominent in the foreground was a feeling of generational unrest in face of the uncertainty of the times, a disorientation now shared with the old-

Josep Maria Jujol, Casa Negre (Sant Joan Despí), 1914-1930.

Josep Maria Jujol, Casa Planells, 1923-1924.

Josep Maria Jujol, plan of Casa Planells, 1923-1924.

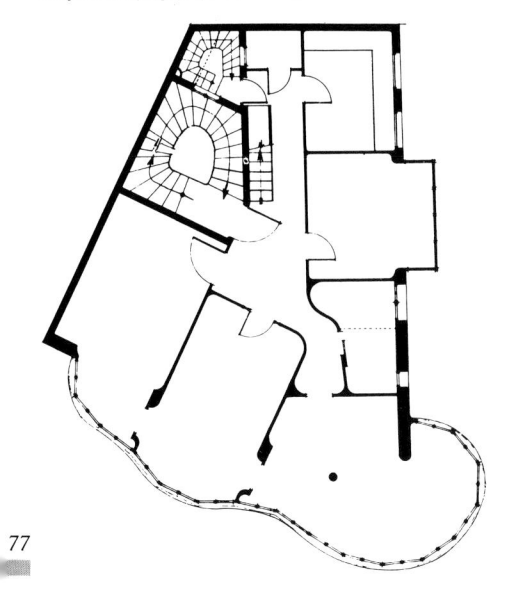

er generation who had been excluded from the *noucentista* mission.

Within this current of revisionism, where individualism was again affirmed, we encounter two contradictory interpretations of a basically Mediterranean idiom. At one end of a range of possibilities deriving from Italian Renaissance examples, especially Brunelleschi's simplified geometry, are Raimon Duran i Reynals (1817-1966), Nicolau Rubió i Tudurí (1891-1981), Josep Goday (1882-1936), Francesc Folguera (1891-1960), Adolf Florensa (1889-1968), etc. At the other extreme of the Renaissance repertoire, where geometry is overtaken by the flowing forms of the Baroque, we encounter Puig i Cadafalch, Manuel Raspall (1877-1937), the architect of La Garriga and Granollers, the Gaudí of the *Sagrada Família*, and the brilliance of Josep Maria Jujol (1879-1949). What linked the individual work of each architect was the transformation of the Mediterranean tradition into a style identifiable as a distinctly Catalan manifestation. The objectives could not have been higher in terms of the ideals which inspired them, where the continuity between *Modernisme* and *Noucentisme* is seen most clearly. But between symbolic Mediterraneanism and late *Modernisme*, these tendencies were doomed to be by-passed and left stranded by the mainline evolution of modern architecture in Europe.

The exception could be Jujol. The force that pushed him to the limits of architectural creativity has left the legacy of an impressive lesson in design. His works were characterized by their successful solution of problems posed by the interaction of his two methods of creation: the juxtaposition of different geometrical systems, and an independent pictorial composition applied to the resulting form. Schematically, we can see the crossing of *Modernisme's* cultural freedom with *noucentista* discipline and control, in creations which give architectural prefigurations of Dada and Surrealism.

The juxtaposition of geometrical systems can be clearly observed in his *Casa Planells* (1924), with the curvilinear façade added on to the regular plan, and in his *Torre de la Creu* (1913-1916) where the merging of five cylinders is regulated by the clean cut of the party wall and other orthogonal divisions. The unity of the cylindrical composition destroys the semi-detached function, which again is set against the curvilinear space inside. This double-game is an original characteristic that sets Jujol's work apart from, and to some extent above, that of Gaudí. The former's achievement is seen to best advantage in what is probably his most accomplished work, the country parish church in Vistabella (1918-1923). It is essentially a building within a building. The spire, in the centre, consists of a pyramid formed by four columns, which in turn support the vaults that rise over the main space. Wrapped around this space is an aisle, with an upward-spiralling roof, supporting steps that can take the visitor from near ground level to the belfry without having to enter the main space of the church. The plan, which is a square, is composed axially along the diagonal, with the entrance at one point and the altar at the other. Jujol's play with the diagonal is found not only in the planning of major elements but also in compositional details, like the fences that surround several of his small houses, from the *Torre San Salvador* (1909) to the *Torre Jujol* (1924) in Sant Joan Despí.

Jujol's other characteristic device is one of architectural graphics, the *esgrafiats* of coloured stucco favoured by both *modernista* and *noucentista* architects for façade decoration. Jujol exploited the technique to far extremes, evolving his highly original 'calligraphic' style which is unmistakable in the whole range of modes in which he employed it, from the most severely regular to the most lyrically baroque. This graphic ornamentation follows its own internal design structure, independent of its supporting

*Francesc Folguera – R. Reventós – M. Utrillo – X. Nogués,
Spanish Village, 1927-1929.*

architecture. Independent but not separated, as we can see when Jujol drew lines of colour casually linking a window to a door or ceiling. The American Venturi's dictum that architecture is in essence a matter of 'decorated sheds' is nowhere more happily exemplified than in this aspect of Jujol's work.

His metalwork is also essencially graphic, with hatched bars contrasting with thin plate strips. The best example is found in the balcony railings of *Casa Milà*, designed in collaboration with Gaudí. The fact is that once one has observed Jujol on his own it is easy to identify his part in collaborations with Gaudí, witness the 'seaweed' balconies and plaster ceilings of the *Casa Milà* or the alterations to the cathedral in Palma, Majorca. It is certainly arguable that Jujol deserves more recognition as a highly original artist, one who took form and pattern and destroyed their normal limits, making them merge together in an architecture that is still extraordinarily stimulating in its relevance to 20th-century currents.

In this sense Jujol must be regarded as literally exceptional. The distance between Catalan architecture and the modern movement in Europe, as it had taken shape by the 1920's, could not have better illustration than in the 1929 International Exhibition buildings on Barcelona's Montjuïc hillside. There the brilliant German pavilion by Mies van der Rohe, with its references to the spatial illusions of De Styl, to the horizontality of Frank Lloyd Wright and, more allusively, back to Schinkel, was in all its abstraction a complete contrast to the heavily monumental *Palau Nacional* by Pere Domènech (1881-1962), P. E. Cendoya (1894-1975) and Enric Catà (1878-1937). Even the severity of the adjoining *Palau Alfons XIII* by Puig looks boring. The utter bankruptcy of Mediterraneanism is seen in the *Palau de l'Agricultura* by Manuel Mayol (1899-1929) and J. M. Ribas (1899-1959), and to a lesser degree in the *Palau de les Arts Gràfi-*

Ludwig Mies van der Rohe, German Pavilion at the International Exhibition, 1929, rebuilt in 1986.

Ludwig Mies van der Rohe, German Pavilion at the International Exhibition, 1929. King Alfonso XIII and Mies van der Rohe at the opening of the Exhibition.

ques by Duran i Reynals and Pelai Martínez (1898). Only a couple of locally designed buildings showed an awareness of European trends. There was the *Artistes Reunits* pavilion (now destroyed) by J. Mestres Fosses (1892-1982) which shared with the fountains and illuminations, inspired by the French architect Jean Forestier (1861-1930), an air of 'art-deco', and then there was the restrained brick architecture of Josep Goday's City of Barcelona pavilion which shows an influence from Amsterdam. The Spanish Village by Francesc Folguera and Ramon Reventós (1892) —with the collaboration of the artists M. Utrillo and Xavier Nogués— introduced the analytical, spatial techniques of Camilio Sitte's city design, whose reputation remains considerable, even on the increase, to this day.

Although it is dangerous to associate artistic and cultural movements too closely with political events, it is obvious that the search for institutional identity, the cultural projection of *Noucentisme*, was badly shaken by political crisis after 1917 and crudely cut off with the advent of Primo de Rivera's dictatorship. The undercurrent of Romantic impulses, however, involving the interplay of individual creativity and collective self-awareness, would not be obliterated. Indeed these forces would re-emerge, renewed and modified, as a historical perspective emerged on the phase of crisis, and as changing circumstances restored the notion of progress into the perceptions of history. The essential change that came about with the advent of the Republic, for the Catalans especially, was to turn that history towards a brave new world of the future. Without its Romantic base, that turn would have been ephemeral.

Carles Forestier – Carles Buïgas, Illuminated Fountains in Montjuïc, 1929.

Francesc Folguera, Casal de Sant Jordi House, 1929-1931.

IV

THE UTOPIAN MODERNS:
A SEARCH FOR IDENTITY IN THE FUTURE

In the same year, 1923, as W.B. Yeats claimed to be the last of the Romantics, Mies van der Rohe wrote: 'We reject all aesthetic speculation, all doctrine, all formalism. Architecture is the will of an epoch translated into space; living, changing, new.' Le Corbusier's articles from *L'Esprit Nouveau* (1919-1922), published as *Vers une architecture* (1925), contain and elaborate upon his famous phrase about the house as a 'machine for living in'. Simplicity, hygiene and an admiration for the functional forms of machinery were the guiding principles expressed in these visionary writings of a self-consciously innovatory movement under the sign of which architecture in Catalonia struck up afresh its dialogue with the most advanced developments on the international scene.

It is easy, even snobbishly fashionable, nowadays to criticize these Utopian pronouncements, and it is easy to blame the destruction of the quality of our built environment on the influence of these pioneers. But the fact is that after the disaster of the First World War the shattered fabric of European society cried out for brave and original solutions of the kind that rationalism held out. It was not that the artists thought that they or their works could transform society, but they consciously inherited a role as safety-valves of social energies and articulators of collective self-interpretations. The visionary theories of the rationalists, then, followed a tradition established by the Romantics. In the second decade of the 20th century, however, the agony of the postwar, the eruption of the Russian Revolution and its threatening reverberations among other national establishments gave dramatic urgency to the question of finding adequate instruments to respond to the requirements of societies in which the 'common good' could no longer satisfy as an empty formula.

Simplicity was required for economy, and economy was indispensable if the fruits of architectural progress were to be available to everyone. Hygiene, in the wake of measures imposed by the authorities to combat the 19th-century legacy of overcrowding and disease, came to enjoy even an exaggerated modishness in claims for air, sun and light. Interest in health in this sense became 'politicized', generating a spate of propaganda and imagery which extolled the hedonistic pleasures of the well-formed figure. The functional forms of machinery figured largely in an 'anti-style' substitution of the composite historicism which was seen to have dominated preceding architectural movements and practice. There was in this evidently something of a moral stance, going back to the 'truthfulness' of Ruskin and looking to the neutrality of the engineer to provide formal solutions to functional problems. It was not, of course, an abolition of style, not even at a purely theoretical level. When it came to actually putting up buildings, architects had to work within their own disciplines, and breaking with the past could never be a simple affair. Historical perspective enables us to now distinguish fine architecture from the vulgar, to recognize the imaginative genius of the individual and his debt to tradition. Nonetheless we are concerned here with a phase in which the Utopian moderns seemed almost to wish to abolish this kind of perspective and to ensure that their achievements (and their inevitable mistakes) be judged by their own standards and criteria.

The Catalan context in which such ideas were first sounded serves particularly to highlight their radical connotations. Neutrality in the European war did nothing to modify the anodyne tone of Catalan society and culture, despite the presence of revolutionary unrest in the streets. The 'vanguard' fervour which had permeated relatively broad social and cultural sectors during the *modernista* epoch was now dulled into a salon elitism. Some exciting exceptions were felt after 1917; various high-level exhibitions brought Paris painting to Barcelona; the visit of Diaghilev's Russian ballet, including Picasso as designer, provided a Parisian counterblast to current Italian and Mediterranean fashion; Josep Dalmau's gallery, founded in 1906, stimulated local artists in contact with a part of the international vanguard displaced by the war, so that the debuts of Salvador Dalí and Joan Miró were geared already to a cosmopolitan ethos. In general, though, Catalonia had slipped out of the modern movement. On the one hand this can be attributed to the restraining effects of *Noucentisme's* concern with order and normality, and the channelling of intellectual efforts into the institutionalization of culture. On the other hand it can be seen too as a consequence of the widening social rift which drove the establishment further to the right, to the extent finally of giving support to the dictatorship of Primo de Rivera. Military success in Morocco in 1925 strengthened Primo's hand, enabling him to ride rough-shod over his Catalan support and to suppress the *Mancomunitat*. Francesc Cambó tried in vain to bridge the gap between Madrid and Barcelona, but the repression encouraged more radical demands from the Catalans, and opinion began to shift towards a Republican solution. In October 1926 Francesc Macià, a retired military officer who had espoused radical politics in face of the *Lliga's* confused conservatism, attempted a colourful armed invasion to liberate Catalonia, only to be stopped by the French police. This climate of uneasiness and political expectation corresponds to the first of the four periods which Oriol Bohigas (*Arquitectura española de la Segunda República*, 1970) identifies and relates to four phases of architectural response to political circumstances. While reminding ourselves again that the rhythms of politics and architecture are never directly synchronized, the development of rationalist architecture in Catalonia can be meaningfully related to a four-stage historical cycle:

1) 1925-1931, boom years for construction, under the confidence fostered by the dictatorship, when even the crash of 1929 had still not made a strong impression in Spain, and when expectations of a Utopian future ran high.
2) 1931-1933, when the Republic gave institutional backing to the rationalists' approach to architecture and town planning.
3) November 1933-February 1936, the *bienio negro*, when right-wing electoral victories put the brakes on buildings and planning projects in the public sector.
4) 1936-1937, from the victory of the Popular Front to the outbreak of the Civil War and the revolutionary circumstances in Catalonia wherein some of the rationalist group were dispersed and others were swept into a revolutionary programme of socialization of the profession and of the construction industry, and municipal take-over of urban property.

Catalonia's dismal contribution in the 1925 International Exhibition of Decoration in Paris, in the form of the *Foment de les Arts Decoratives* stand, was recognized by the president of the FAD, Santiago Marco: 'We were discreet... We could not, frankly, expect more.' He lamented Gaudí's refusal to participate and noted the paradox that Art-Deco should appear exotic to a country which had previously accepted the innovations of that artist. In addition it should be remembered that it was for this same exhibition that Le Corbusier built his famous *Esprit Nouveau* pavilion.

Suggestive references to the new architecture are found in both Rafael Benet's ambiguous writings in the journal *La Ciutat i la Casa* (1925-1927) and Nicolau Rubió's book *Diàlegs sobre l'arquitectura* (1927). But it was probably the articles by the Madrid architect García Mercadal (1896-1985) in the journal *Arquitectura*, between 1927 and 1929, that created the greatest impact among the students and young architects. García Mercadal had spent the period 1921-1927 travelling around Europe, working in Germany with the expressionist Poelzig and making contact there with the eclectic func-

Le Corbusier – GATCPAC, Macià Plan (drawing by Josep Torres Clavé), 1932-1934.

Le Corbusier – GATCPAC, Macià Plan (redrawn by X. Monteys), 1932-1934.

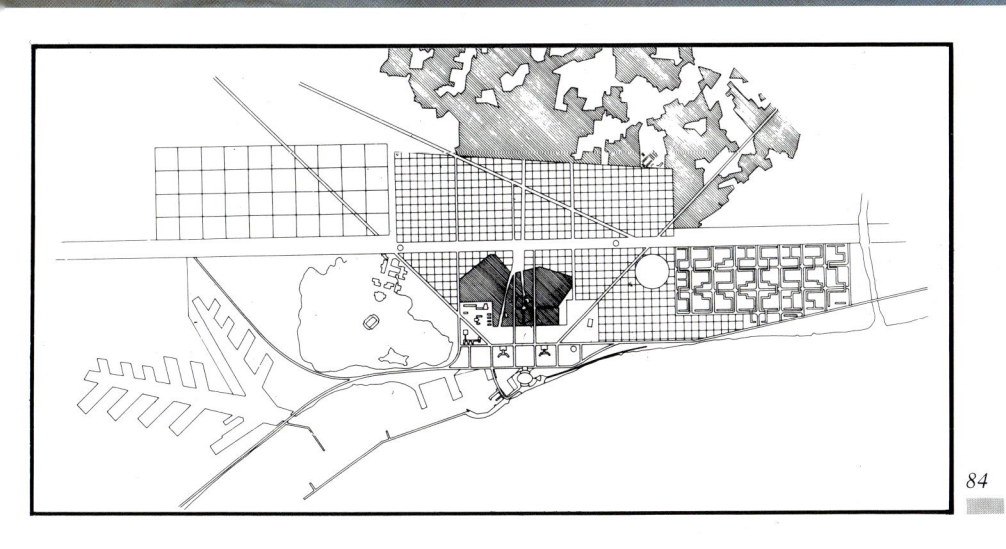

Francesc Folguera, Casal de Sant Jordi House, 1929-1931.

tionalist Behrens. He also met Mies van der Rohe and the group associated with *L'Esprit Nouveau*. In Madrid he organized talks by Le Corbusier, Gropius, Theo van Doesburg, Mendelsohn and others. When asked to design a monument to Goya in Saragossa he threatened to resign unless given a free hand. Instead of producing the traditional figurative grouping, he changed the brief (the brief or programme being the starting point of functionalism in modern architecture) into plans for what he called the *Rincón de Goya*, consisting of a pavilion opening on to a park and housing a library and small museum of the painter's life and work. This was indisputably the first fully-fledged modern rationalist construction in Spain (1927-1928). It was followed by the vast project for the University City of Madrid (1927), collaboration in which was a kind of initiation to rationalism for many young architects. In June 1928 García Mercadal was invited to the now famous meeting in the castle of La Sarraz in Switzerland, where all the avant-garde of European architecture gathered to coordinate the international struggle for the new architecture. They formed the parent organization of CIRPAC *(Comité International pour la Réalisation des Problèmes Architecturaux Contemporains)* which planned future meetings under the letters CIAM.

The Catalans were not long in responding to the initiatives taken in Madrid. Le Corbusier, invited to the Spanish capital in May 1928, was 'intercepted' by a telegram from Josep Lluís Sert (1902-1983) who arranged for him to be met at Barcelona station by a group of young architects and whisked off to give a spontaneous lecture. It was an indication of how ready was the Catalan terrain to receive the seeds of the new architecture.

The first major buildings in Barcelona to pick up the new styling were the Myrurgia cosmetics factory (1928-1930) by Antoni Puig i Gairalt (1887-1935) and the block of flats at a corner of

Francesc Folguera, Casal de Sant Jordi House, 1929-1931.

the carrer Lleida (1928) by Ramon Reventós (1892-1959). The innovative feature in each case is the play on vertical and horizontal emphases in the façades, even though the classical axial dominance is retained.

The background to these developments contained various signs of renewed artistic vitality and polemical aggresion. The futurist *Yellow Manifesto* (1928), signed by Dalí, Lluís Montanyà and Sebastià Gasch —a painter, a writer and a critic— denounced the sterility and negativeness of the established Catalan culture, proclaiming that the future lay in the spirit of the latest machinery, the cinema, jazz, beauty competitions, transatlantic liners, airports, etc., including 'una arquitectura d'avui', an architecture for today. While they were being accused of snobbery and even fascism, Miró and Dalí were meanwhile consolidating international reputations, and the surrealist film *Un chien andalou*, filmed in Cadaqués by Buñuel and Dalí, gave a real thrill to the progressive circles in Paris in 1929. Within the combative atmosphere it is not surprising that the young Catalan architects should stage a counter-exhibition in the Galeries Dalmau on the eve of the 1929 International Exhibition in Montjuïc, the latter being dominated by the monumental state architecture of the Primo de Rivera regime. In the unofficial exhibition works by Sert, Torres (1906-1938), Rodríguez, Yllescas (b.1903) and others aroused considerable public interest, and the project for Barcelona airport by Puig i Gairalt was a major attraction, coinciding with Ramon Argiles' and Pere Benavent's (1899-1974) project for a futurist bridge over the Llobregat river. One immediate consequence of the exhibition was the formation of GATCPAC *(Grup d'Artistes i Tècnics Catalans per al Progrés de l'Arquitectura Contemporània)*, an obvious replica of CIRPAC, initiated by Sert, Yllescas and three other architects who worked in the same building, Germà Rodríguez (1900-1963), Ricard Churruca (b.1902) and Francesc Fàbregas

Antoni Puig Gairalt, Myrurgia Factory, 1928-1930.

Antoni Puig Gairalt, Myrurgia Factory, 1928-1930.

(1901-1942). Sert had set up his office with Sixt Yllescas in 1929, but spent much time away in Paris working with Le Corbusier. During this time Yllescas built his Vilaró house near the *Parc Güell,* known as the 'ship house' *(Casa de la Barca)* on account of its obvious nautical lines. Situated on a steep hillside, the entrance is set on the upper floor where the living-room has a sweeping curved terrace above the slit windows of the bedrooms below. For his part, Sert designed a block of flats in the carrer Rosselló (1930) between party walls. But their main project, in collaboration and involving other members of the GATCPAC, was the launching of the idea of a 'parallel city' for recreation close to Barcelona in Gavà and Castelldefels. The precise form of the project and the political strategy for its development were to be major issues in the first years of the Republic.

The 1929 Exhibition had no impact on the young rationalist group, in spite of displaying two pavilions by Mies van der Rohe: his famous empty one and the less well known Electrical Supply pavilion consisting of a large, plain, blind box. Two local architects who were involved —Reventós with the Spanish Village and the two italianate entrance towers, and Folguera also with the Spanish Village— were already engaged with designing, elsewhere, buildings of a quite different inspiration, much closer to the spirit and image of the new architecture. This fact illustrates that one need not be a 'young Turk' to be receptive to the new style or 'anti-style'. The way in which these and other architects brought their classical training and professional experience to the service of architectural progress in its rationalist guise gave to the new architecture in Catalonia a maturity which was perhaps missing in other countries. By being less aggressively iconoclastic it managed to be more thoroughly advanced than in some other European countries in which tradition had less to offer.

Francesc Folguera (1891-1960) designed and

Sixt Yllescas, Casa Vilaró, 1929.

Ramon Reventós, Apartments in carrer Lleida, 1928.

built the *Casal de Sant Jordi* (1929-1931) on the corner of the carrer de Casp and the Via Laietana. Clearly influenced by German expressionism and, as Bohigas notes, anticipating the functionalist concepts of the *Moderne Bauformen*, this is a building which appeared independently of the GATCPAC movement and yet, with is stark unorthodox appearance, could be mistaken today for an edifice put up in the 1960's. Apart from the simplicity of its plain walls and volume, its originality is in the distribution of the windows which not only increase in size from top to bottom (reminiscent of Gaudí's *Casa Batlló*) but have four clearly different rhythms according to the functional use of the floor. The first two storeys house the commercial activities normal to any central-Barcelona building, and are really only openings between the structural pillars. The next three floors are for smaller offices with a run of standard windows that can be read as three lines of strip fenestration. Above these are three floors of paired windows, two pairs of which form corner openings; these correspond to floors occupied by dwellings. The upper floor contains only seven horizontal windows placed between two floating slabs easily distinguished by the ventilation holes. The uppermost floor forms part of the private accommodation of the owners, and contains the bedrooms, all facing inwards off the street towards the south and protected from the street noise by a corridor. These bedrooms look on to a private roof-garden terrace away from the street. The composition of the façade is completed with the introduction of four protruding bays that run up through six floors, picking out the horizontal dimension of the composition. The complex effects of this conformation, using simple elements, as well as providing one of the more satisfactory solutions to problems posed by Cerdà's cut-off corners of the Barcelona city block, are to be seen as the coming of age of the new architecture in its Catalan context.

Josep Goday, Collasso i Gil School, 1932.

Josep Lluís Sert – Sixt Yllescas,
Apartment block in carrer Muntaner, 1930-1931.

During the confused and critical final months of the reign of Alfonso XIII, at the beginning of 1931, contacts were strengthened between rationalist architects working in various parts of Spain. First there was the March meeting in association with the exhibition at the Gran Casino in San Sebastián, and then Sert and Mercadal organized the October meeting in Saragossa where the GATEPAC was founded. The C of GATCPAC was changed to E for *Españoles*, and the formation was immediately admitted as the Spanish section of CIRPAC. Even though the ambit was now the whole of Spain, the dynamo or ginger group continued to be the Catalan contingent.

Apart from these organizational occasions, which were of fundamental importance in tying the work of the Spaniards to the main European current, the buildings produced at this time worked out the first concerted exercises in the new architectural medium. The duplex flats in the carrer Muntaner by Sert and Yllescas (1930-1931) show an impressively high level of good detailed design, over and above the wilful innovation of two-storey dwellings piled on top of one another. One has the impression that the façade was designed first and the plan fitted as best it could be, for the terraces correspond to a narrow gallery *above* the living room and not to the floor level as would be expected. Attention is also attracted by the light green colouring of the rendered surface, almost certainly to reduce the glare of white conventionally used throughout central Europe. Rodríguez's use of pale pink for his flats in the Via Augusta had probably the same motive. The latter example shows a further interesting variation in that it rejects symmetry in favour of shifting the balcony terraces to face the sun.

Meanwhile there were developments among non-GATEPAC architects whose resistance to Utopian ideals was by now beginning to be looked upon as 'anti-style', an indication of how the

Joaquim Lloret, Barraquer Clinic, 1936-1939.

Joaquim Lloret, Barraquer Clinic, 1936-1939.

novelties of rationalism were being accepted and 'normalized'. The offices for the publishers Seix i Barral (1930-1931) by Jaume Mestres (1892-1981), now demolished, comprised a heavy eclectic expressionist façade of brick and stucco, while in the same architect's Blanquerna school in the Via Augusta (1930-1933) the façade presents a more neutral modernity. It is worth considering these two as cases of buildings which are given a modern air only by epidermic effects of styling, devoid of Utopian connotations and content.

The Utopian spirit, though, was undoubtedly abroad, and assertively so, on the political front as the new decade was entered. In the municipal elections of April 1931 the *Esquerra Republicana* party, founded by Macià and Lluís Companys, scored sweeping victories over the now discredited *Lliga*. Macià was encouraged to declare a Catalan Republic within a Federal Spain. The subsequent moderation of this to the formula of an autonomous *Generalitat* within the Spanish Republic was a compromise which reconciled idealism with political realities. The Utopian momentum was not lost in the compromise, and was appropriately expressed in architectural terms. A second phase of rationalism was entered upon in which the new architecture was projected within a positive framework of development plans under the aegis of the public institutions.

We should remark that the Catalan situation in this regard was unique in Europe. Although the city authorities in Berlin and Frankfurt were responsible for the rationalist architecture of the new districts, with unprecedented public housing undertakings, these were cases of the 'circumstantial' extension of architecture into mass housing, promoting necessary relationships between the profession and the cities. Utopian theories about new cities abounded, based on the *tabula rasa* theory ('Architecture or Revolution', which Le Corbusier had written in the early 1920's), but the circumstances for a full-scale application were few and far between. The 'revolutionary' situation of Catalonia in 1931 offered the potential of just such a *tabula rasa*, and the will to exploit it was there, with a strong nationalistic justification. The charismatic zeal of Francesc Macià was combined with the keen organizational abilities of his military background, to unify the energies of Republicans, Socialists and the influential anarchist trades union, the CNT. There was momentarily created the spirit of a nation 'born again', fired by the ideal of a Brave New World. And the architects of the GATCPAC offered proposals for the concrete realization of Utopian theory. The significance of this coordination of social and architectural projects must be stressed, because it has been underappreciated by history, cast into the shadows first by the absorbing events of the Civil War and then by World War II. The Anglo-Saxon, German and Italian bias of international architectural history has overlooked the key contribution of Spain, in particular of Catalonia, to this major chapter in the story of the modern movement.

Regional planning, a parallel city, a development plan for the historic heart of Barcelona, the integration of the block-dwelling concept into the city texture of streets and squares, the adaptation of functional requirements to climatic conditions: all these and other imaginative ideas were proposed and put into effect within the short life of the Republic, and with the full backing and encouragement of the institutional authorities. So much would never have been undertaken and achieved without the solid commitment of the professionals —doctors, lawyers, etc. as well as architects and planners— to the common political cause. The collaborative and associational tendencies of Catalan civil society, cemented by its strong sense of linguistic and cultural identity, are recognized as integral features of its 'differential' character. Under the Republic, where the link between progress and national identity was strongly reaffirmed, the common commitment surged most powerfully. The collective work of the architects, always naturally inclined to involvement in social projects, was intensified in the service of a Catalonia governed by its own progressive forces within a progressive Spain.

Collaboration between Sert and J. Torres Clavé had begun with the project for the coastal holiday village presented at the Galeries Dalmau exhibition in 1929. These two forceful figures were the natural leaders of the Catalan GATEPAC group which also included M. Subiño (1904-1984), C. Alzamora (1905-1975), G. Rodríguez, R. Churruca, P. Armengou (b.1905), S. Yllescas, F. Perales (1905-1956), and later J. Subirana (1904-1978), R. Ribas (b.1907), J. González (b.1906), R. Duran Reynals, and Antoni Bonet (b.1913). Their collective energies coalesced in the publication of the journal *GATEPAC, AC (Documentos de Actividad Contemporánea)* whose first issue came out before the April 1931 elections and the last one, number 25, in June 1937. A journal for its times, then, which denounced not only the hypocrisy of decadent classical decorativeness in architecture but also the scandalous social conditions of the city. Its articles gave balanced coverage to the work of modern architects abroad and to the range of new developments at home, with a special monographic issue being devoted to such themes as schools and education. Also on the eve of the 1931 elections the group opened a furniture shop on the Passeig de Gràcia, MIDVA (*Mobles i Decoració per a la Vivenda Actual* — furniture and decoration for today's homes). As well as being a permanent exhibition of modern furniture and building materials, it was the meeting and working centre for a group of architects inspired by a social and artistic mission.

Work continued apace on the *Ciutat de Repòs* at Castelldefels, giving shape to Le Corbusier's theories for a green city with vertical buildings. This was just one front of the activities. Attention was also turned, inevitably, to the problems of expansion and renovation of the city of Barcelona itself. The skill and sensitivity applied here have to be appraised not only in theoretical terms but also, as Solà-Morales emphasizes, in terms of the regard shown for practical feasibility. The *Pla Macià* was anything but a pipedream.

Le Corbusier made a third visit to Barcelona in the Spring of 1932, for a meeting to organize the IV congress of CIRPAC. Originally planned for Moscow, the congress took place instead in 1933 on the yacht *Paris II*, sailing in the Mediterranean, where the famous Athens Charter on the functional city was drawn up. The GATEPAC contributions —the plan for the recreational city and the *Pla Macià* for Barcelona— were fundamental documents for the working sessions in which Sert, Torres, Ribas and Bonet participated actively, the preparations for which had involved the cream of the European rationalist movement, Le Corbusier, Bourgeois, Giedion, Gropius, Breuer, Pollini, Steiger, etc.

The most important aspect of the Macià Plan was its effort to provide an overall solution to Barcelona's problems after the abuses perpetrated on the original *Pla Cerdà*. It recognized the new demands made by new social factors and accordingly worked on the basis of a classification/distribution defined by different uses: production, dwellings, civic centres, recreation and communication. The plan also proposed expanding the Cerdà 133m × 133m block to a super-block of 400m × 400m, the renovation of the old part of the city and incorporation of the parallel city for recreation. Although not officially commissioned by the *Generalitat*, the scheme was encouraged by its patronage, and by that of the municipal council, and was exhibited to the public in 1934. As a result of these initiatives, the *Generalitat* officially commissioned through its

GATCPAC, Casa Bloc, 1932-1936.

Le Corbusier at the Palau de la Generalitat in 1932 during a meeting of the CIRPAC, directive committee of the CIAM.

105

Francesc Folguera, Casa del Llorà (Collsacabra), 1935.

Patronat de l'Habitació the *Casa Bloc* (1932-1936), which was in effect an essay in how the superblocks or *immobles-viles* could be designed. The architects first decided on a duplex flat in order to concentrate the access, with open galleries leading from the minimum number of lifts and staircases, and to avoid enclosed lightwells. The corridor gallery access encouraged communication between neighbours as a kind of neighbourhood-street replica. Some basic dwelling units were first put up in an experimental row just next to the site to ensure that the nucleus of the living-unit really worked. In fact, as a result of tests, plans were modified to concentrate the water-using areas together, forming a protective barrier for the intimacy of the dwelling and at the same time allowing the kitchen to control the wide corridor-street in front of the house. A deep sun-terrace was provided on the opposite side. The upstairs bedrooms were interlocked with those next door in such a way that a variable mixture of two-, three- and four- bedroomed houses could be arranged. The super-block itself was articulated about the vertical accesses to form a Z figure, so that the whole construction was organized as a single unit, like the Viennese *hofs* built in the 1920's, and formed at the same time façades to the existing streets while creating new urban space within itself. There was one such area that was open to the street, occupied by a small nursery school, while the other, turned away from the street, housed small workshops and community facilities. We have here, then, a revolutionary break away from the enclosed island blocks, a scheme which preserved the advantages of the *hofs* while avoiding the pitfalls of the hygienic slab blocks proposed by the *Bauhaus* and Le Corbusier that have created so much damage in the post-war years in and around our cities.

The *Casa-Bloc* concept itself constitutes a rational departure from *tabula-rasa* theories, ac-

Josep Lluís Sert – J. Torres Clavé, Week-end Houses in Garraf, 1935.

knowledging practical realities and being designed to fit into the existing city context. The introduction of the idea of mixed uses, either in the autonomous village or in the *immoble-vila* within the city, was taken from Le Corbusier, but it was also something which corresponded to the mixed-use reality of Barcelona itself. The interpreters of the *Pla Macià* thus showed a realistic flexibility in the face of the advantages and disadvantages of the environment they were out to improve. The experimental building was unfortunately never occupied by the working families for whom it was intended. At the end of the Civil War it was taken over by the army who proceded to disfigure the design by infilling the open sides. Only very recently, with that particular chapter of barbarism ended, have complete restoration and eventual civilian occupation become real possibilities. It would be a most fitting tribute to its authors and to the movement to which they were committed.

As an indication of the concerted scope within which such projects were conceived and undertaken, we should note here the importance of N. Rubió's initial study for a Regional Plan of Catalonia *(Pla de Distribució de Zones del Territori Català)* commissioned by the *Generalitat* in 1931. Eventually published in 1932, it can be considered as one of the first of its type in Europe. The *Generalitat* also created a commission to chart the territorial division of Catalonia, based on verifiable geographical and economic criteria, to supersede the arbitrary and cumbersome division of the Spanish provinces. This work, also initiated in 1931, was approved by the *Generalitat* in 1936. Although the Franco regime cut short and tried to obliterate this territorial mapping, it survives to this day and, rehabilitated, forms the basis of today's political thought and discussion. It is yet another positive legacy of the collaboration between architecture, planning and government during the Republic.

While the GATEPAC architects were breaking

Josep Lluís Sert – J. Torres Clavé – Joan B. Subirana, Antitubercular Clinic, 1934-1938.

new ground at home, with high-level international recognition, it was still almost inevitable that they should encounter some local opposition. It would be wrong to underestimate the influence of those Catalan architects who, perpetuating *noucentista* values, admitted in theory and in practice the existence of the modern movement, but rejected its Utopian overtones and sought to reconcile it with tradition in order that the sense of local identity should not be sacrificed to internationalism. Among them stands Josep Goday whose Collasso i Gil school (1932) was designed after the author's visit to Scandinavia. It is an interesting case of honest synthesis. The plan follows Goday's *noucentista* schools of the 1920's, with the maximum elimination of the corridor introducing large auxiliary communal spaces. The L shaped building on its corner site retains a classical composition of masses, but the surface is treated with an intelligent detailing of dark brick, with windows grouped together in carefully separated but correlated horizontal and vertical strips. Goday was too sensitive a practitioner not to learn from his travels and from contemporary developments, giving in this case a modified application of expressionist techniques.

Pere Benavent, infilling with a block of flats between party walls, in the Avinguda Gaudí, followed the *Bauhaus* vocabulary (as did Sert with his building in the carrer Rosselló), but can be seen to have deliberately *translated* it into what he considered the spirit of national identity. His use of brick and the classical-looking disposition of the windows, avoiding compositional unity with the terraces, conform to a strenuous effort to avoid facile repetition of Le Corbusier's recipes. Bohigas points this out, and he also ironically remarks that Benavent, despite all his denunciations of architectural imitations (archaeology), be they of the 13th century or of the 1920's, was not an exponent of 'pure and simple architecture' nor of the

Josep Lluís Sert – J. Torres Clavé – Joan B. Subirana,
Antitubercular Clinic, 1934-1938.

'immortal spirit' as he would have liked, but rather an architect influenced by the contents of the journal *Moderne Bauformen*.

Internal tensions were already testing the Republic with the elections of November 1933 and the right-wing victory, in Spain as a whole, of Lerroux's Radicals supported by Gil Robles and the CEDA (an electoral confederation of Catholic parties). The left, though, retained power in Catalonia, with Companys assuming the Presidency of the *Generalitat* after Macià's death in December 1933. Relations between Barcelona and Madrid now became more strained than ever, and positions were polarized in terms that prefigured the radical confrontation of the Civil War. The revolt of October 1934, intended to be a blow for a Catalan State (at a time of other challenges to counter-revolution in the Republic), went off at half-cock, resulting in the imprisonment of Companys and suspension of the *Generalitat's* powers until the Popular Front victory in February 1936.

There was thus a vacuum of political authority in Catalonia which lasted 19 months, during which time the GATEPAC was orphaned of official support. Before this crisis, however, in February 1934, after previous studies in 1933, the *Generalitat's Departament de Sanitat i Assistència Social* commissioned Sert, Torres and Subirana to design the *Dispensari Central Antituberculós* (1934-1938), the finest building to emerge from the GATEPAC and one of the most perfect and most mature rationalist constructions in contemporary Europe. Like so much GATEPAC work, this building was displaced by war from the annals of modern archictecture, and its status is only now being fully appreciated. The *Dispensari* is a steel-framed, L shaped building that encloses a courtyard, an area forming an open-air 'hall' from which the patients have direct access to the different departments. The architects fully exploited the advantages of Mediterranean weather to do away with the sort of indoor hall which would have been appropriate and conventional in a northern climate, substituting here a traditional entrance courtyard so typical of the medieval houses and palaces of Barcelona. One arm of the L shaped building contains the consulting rooms on the three upper floors. These are arranged facing northwards, with the corridor on the south side protecting these rooms from the excessive summer heat, thus inverting the distributional values found elsewhere in Europe. High strip windows run along these passages which are also punctuated with occasional viewing panels at eye-level. The end wall is covered with fibrous cement sheets expressing the temporary nature of the ending of this wing which could be extended as necessary. The green ceramic tiles of the recessed ground floor are a reminder of the functional use of this material by the architects of *Modernisme*. The other wing houses a small lecture-theatre on the top floor, built parallel to the main wing of consulting rooms. The shape of this little lecture-theatre has determined the form and distribution of the floors below, but such constraints as this imposed are overcome. The meticulous attention to all aspects of design makes this building a miniature repertoire of the language of modern architecture. History, however, has set in relief the tragic fate of the Utopianism which informed it. War, exile and death for a long time obscured its spirit and significance. Sert escaped to America; Torres was killed in action in the front against Franco. Subirana supervised the construction through war and revolution.

The importance of the *Dispensari* for the modern movement in architecture is that it anticipated the functional requirements of a society and culture whose need to affirm identity was powerful and constant. It is a building that is both unmistakably abreast of its times, fully modern in this sense, and at the same time unequivocally Catalan.

Its character, within the rationalist idiom, is inexplicable except in terms of local points of reference: the simplicity and structural honesty of Catalan Gothic, epitomized in the church of Santa Maria del Mar; the domestic humanity and functional aggregation of *Modernisme*; *Noucentisme's* classical control of form and façades. Fifty years on we can now see this clearly, because our contemporary exponents of Modernism have at last assimilated all these terms within their own rich vocabulary of design. When Catalan culture repudiates the mean conservatism of an excess of *seny*, when it can breathe its history fresh, with native innocence, open to the world, as in the work of an artist like Joan Miró, it has the uncanny knack of producing revolutionary works of art of worldwide significance. Its architecture of the 1930's precariously achieved this level.

After the failure of the October revolt and the suspension of the *Generalitat*, there were no more public commissions. This gave Sert and Torres the opportunity to design two week-end houses at Garraf to the south of Barcelona. They were simple rectangular plans roofed with the Catalan vault and set upon a rubble stone base. Here we have for the first time the fusion of popular constructions with the modern rational idiom, in the same year that Le Corbusier himself introduced similar Mediterranean elements into his own work. Such non-dogmatic openness was possible only in the hands of top-rate architects. These houses, now unfortunately disfigured, are reminders that the influence was not all one-way, and that Catalan architecture made a positive input into the development of the international modern movement.

Other buildings of note from this third phase of rationalist architecture are the *Joieria Roca* (1934) by Sert on the commanding corner of the Gran Via-Passeig de Gràcia; G. Rodríguez's flats and Astoria cinema (1933-1934) in the carrer París; the block of flats by Yllescas (1934) in the

Raimon Duran Reynals,
Apartments in carrer Aribau-Camp d'en Vidal, 1934.

carrer Pàdua; the dazzling white block (1934) in the carrer Aribau by Duran Reynals, where we find first introduced the deep terrace which was to be such a ubiquitous feature of post-war housing. It is worth commenting on two other buildings which were the work of architects on the margins of the GATEPAC circle. Francesc Folguera's *El Llorà* house (1935) in Collsacabra uses plain surfaces with effects reminiscent of Loos, while the *Clínica Barraquer* (1936-1939) by Joaquim Lloret (b.1890), even more an outsider, owes more to the German expressionism of Mendelsohn and Art-Deco than to the GATEPAC's advanced example.

On July 18, 1936, provoked ostensibly by the assassination of the traditionalist leader Calvo Sotelo, the forces of reaction struck back with a military revolt which spread from Morocco to the garrison towns on the mainland. Hesitation and miscalculation on both sides allowed the rebel generals and the government to consolidate their forces. A protracted civil war was inevitable. The direct ravages of military campaigns did not hit Catalonia for two years, but Catalan society was deeply affected by the sharply revolutionary swing of the Popular Front forces that were divided in their interpretations, sometimes with uncontrolled violence, as to how the circumstances could best be put to the service of the Revolution, or as to whether the first priority was Revolution or the salvation of the Republic. Companys, as the reinstated President, did his best to ride the storm. The GATEPAC was bound to be caught up in the contradictions of the situation, as Solà-Morales has indicated. As a movement whose Utopianism was already heavily committed (with a few notable exceptions) to the cause of the Republic, inseparable from that of progressive Catalanism, the group geared itself in the final stages to a dynamic of change that only a few architects would agree to follow.

With Sert in exile, Torres Clavé took over the

leadership. Within the collectivist political direction that the *Generalitat* had taken, the building industry was reorganized for controlled economic production. The professional association of architects was incorporated in 1936 into a fully unified syndicate of all building workers. Torres and F. Fàbregas coordinated this development. The *Generalitat* pushed ahead with its plan to collectivize urban property by creating a *Comissariat de l'Estatge* in 1936; rent payments were suspended in January 1937, prior to the decree for the municipalization of urban property in the June of that year. Meanwhile the architects' union, together with the students, worked out a new plan of studies adapted to the requirements of the new society that was being forged in the revolutionary conflagration. In the same area, the *Comitè de l'Escola Nova* (CENU) put forward intelligent plans for the transformation of existing religious and commercial properties into schools built and equipped to proper standards. This imaginative alternative to purpose-built accommodation was extremely enlightened, but it created problems beyond the formal capacity of the practitioners involved. It is sadly ironic that the Utopian adventure should end in such frustration and in such tragic circumstances.

During the Civil War two exhibitions were held abroad, each side in the conflict patronizing its own: the Republic in Paris, 1937, and the inconsequential effort promoted by the rebels in Venice, 1938. Sert, together with Luis Lacasa (1899-1966), designed the pavilion for the Republican government at the Paris exhibition. An exposed steel-frame building formed one side of a square court covered with canvas slung between cables. External curved ramps and staircases gave access to an enclosed upper level, while the ground floor was left open as a porch. Here, at one end, was the famous *Guernica* by Picasso. The same artist also exhibited a sculpture and this was in the company of other major contributions from Catalonia: *Montserrat* by Juli González and Joan Miró's *El pagès català i la revolució*. Both as an exhibition pavilion, with its static spaces and simply controlled circulation, and as a building object in itself, mellowing the international style with a strongly Mediterranean spatial freedom, this is an architectural achievement that merits at least the same sort of attention from critics and historians as that devoted to the Mies pavilion in the 1929 Barcelona exhibition. Is it too idealistic to ask why it too should not be rebuilt? And why not in Madrid, to house again *Guernica* as it was originally exhibited? It would be a way of doing justice to a vision of Utopia that is now being recovered and recognized as a key phase of Catalan involvement in a total history whose coordinates were neither strictly Catalan nor even Spanish, but truly international.

The cruel interruption of the Civil War and the defeat of democracy in 1939 left a gap in this local contribution to the evolution of the Modern Movement. The complex processes of post-war recovery and the renewed struggle to affirm identity and to evince modernity are now being seen not as a separate but as a continuing story that others perhaps will be better placed to tell.

Josep Lluís Sert – Luis Lacasa, Pavilion of the Republican Government at the Paris Exhibition, 1937.

Josep Lluís Sert – Luis Lacasa, Pavilion of the Republican Government at the Paris Exhibition, 1937.

102

103

LOCATION OF BUILDINGS MENTIONED IN THE TEXT

BENAVENT, Pere:
- Flats (1933)
Av. de Gaudí, 56. Barcelona.

BERENGUER, Francesc:
- Wine-cellar in Garraf (1888-1890)
Carretera Comarcal, 246. Garraf (Garraf).

- Mercat de la Llibertat (1893)
Plaça de la Llibertat, 186. Barcelona.

BUÏGAS, Gaietà:
- Naval Pavilion (1929)
Now demolished.

BUÏGAS, Carles:
- Montjuïc lights and fountains (1929)
(in collaboration with Forestier, J.)
Av. de la Reina Maria Cristina, Montjuïc. Barcelona.

CATÀ, Enric:
- Palau Nacional (1929)
(in collaboration with Domènech, P. and Cendoya, P.E.)
Mirador del Palau. Montjuïc. Barcelona.

CERDÀ, Ildefons:
- First residential building (1863) of Cerdà plan
Carrer del Consell de Cent/carrer Llúria. Barcelona.

CENDOYA, P.E.:
- Palau Nacional (1929)
(in collaboration with Catà, E. and Domènech, P.)
Mirador del Palau. Montjuïc. Barcelona.

CORNET, Josep:
- Born Market (1873-1876)
(in collaboration with Fontserè, J. and Rovira, A.)
Carrer del Comerç, 29. Barcelona.

- Sant Antoni Market (1876-1882)
(in collaboration with Rovira, A.)
Carrer del Comte d'Urgell, 1. Barcelona.

DOMÈNECH, Pere:
- Palau Nacional (1929)
(in collaboration with Cendoya, P.E. and Catà, E.)
Mirador del Palau, Montjuïc. Barcelona.

DOMÈNECH I ESTAPÀ, Josep:
- Model Prison (1881-1904)
Carrer d'Entença, 155. Barcelona.

- Science Academy (1883)
Rambles, 115. Barcelona.

- Palau de Justícia (1887-1908)
(in collaboration with Sagnier, E.)
Av. de Lluís Companys, 16. Barcelona.

- Catalana de Gas i Electricitat (1893-1895)
Av. del Portal de l'Angel, 20. Barcelona.

- Hospital Clínic (1904)
Carrer Casanova, 143. Barcelona.

- Fabra Observatory (1904)
Tibidabo. Barcelona.

- Casa Cucurella (1911)
Carrer de Villarroel, 62. Barcelona.

DOMÈNECH I MONTANER, Lluís:
- Editorial Montaner i Simon (1880)
Carrer d'Aragó, 255. Barcelona.

- Café-Restaurant (1887-1888)
Parc de la Ciutadella. Barcelona. (Now Zoological museum)

- International Hotel (1888)
Now demolished.

- Casa Thomas (1895-1898)
Carrer de Mallorca, 291-293. Barcelona.

- The Pere Mata mental hospital (1897-1919)
Reus (Baix Camp).

- Casa Navàs (1901)
Plaça d'Espanya, 7. Reus (Baix Camp).

- Hospital de Sant Pau (1902-1910)
Av. de Sant Antoni Maria Claret, 167-171. Barcelona.

- Casa Lleó Morera (1905)
Passeig de Gràcia, 35. Barcelona.

- Palau de la Música Catalana (1905-1908)
Plaça d'Amadeu Vives, 1. Barcelona.

- Casa Fuster (1908-1910)
Passeig de Gràcia, 132. Barcelona

DURAN REYNALS, R.:
- Palau de les Arts Gràfiques (1929)
(in collaboration with Martínez, P.)
Passeig de Santa Madrona. Montjuïc. Barcelona.
(Now Archaeological museum).

- Flats (1934)
Carrer d'Aribau, 243 and Camp d'en Vidal, 16. Barcelona.

FALQUÉS, Pere:
- Agricultural pavilion (1929)
Now demolished.

FERRÉS, E.:
- Casa Ferrer-Vidal (1916)
Passeig de Gràcia, 114. Barcelona.

FOLGUERA, Francesc:
- The Spanish Village (1927-1929)
(in collaboration with Reventós, R., Utrillo, M. and Nogués, X.)
Av. del Marqués de Comillas. Montjuïc. Barcelona.

- Casal de Sant Jordi (1929-1931)
Carrer de Pau Claris/carrer de Casp. Barcelona.

- Casa del Llorà (1935)
Collsacabra (Osona).

FONTSERÈ, Josep:
- Umbracle
Parc de la Ciutadella. Passeig de Picasso. Barcelona.

- Born Market (1873-1876)
(in collaboration with Cornet, J. and Rovira, A.)
Carrer del Comerç, 29. Barcelona.

- Water deposit building.
Carrer Wellington. Barcelona.

FORESTIER, J.:
- Montjuïc lights and fountains (1929)
(in collaboration with Buïgas, C.)
Av. de la Reina Maria Cristina, Montjuïc. Barcelona.

GATCPAC
- Casa Bloc (1932-1936)
Av. de Torres i Bages, 91-105. Sant Andreu. Barcelona.

GAUDÍ, Antoni:
- Casa Vicens (1883-1885)
Carrer de les Carolines, 24. Barcelona.

- El Capricho (1883-1885)
Comillas (Santander).

- Sagrada Família (1884-1926)
Carrer de la Marina, 251-253. Barcelona.

- Palau Güell (1885-1889)
Carrer Nou de la Rambla, 3. Barcelona.

- Güell gatehouse and stables (1887)
Av. de Pedralbes, 77. Barcelona.

- Col·legi de Santa Teresa (1889-1894)
Carrer de Ganduxer, 85-105.
Barcelona.

- Colònia Güell Church (1898-1915)
Santa Coloma de Cervelló (Baix Llobregat).

- Bellesguard (1900-1902)
Carrer Bellesguard, 16-20. Barcelona.

- Parc Güell (1900-1914)
Carrer d'Olot. Barcelona.

- Casa Batlló (1905-1907)
Passeig de Gràcia, 43. Barcelona.

- Casa Milà 'La Pedrera' (1905-1911)
Passeig de Gràcia, 92. Barcelona.

GODAY, Josep:
- Grup escolar 'Baixeras' (1918-1922)
Via Laietana, 11. Barcelona.

- Grup escolar 'Lluís Vives' (1918-1922)
Carrer de Canalejas, 107. Barcelona.

- Grup escolar 'Milà i Fontanals' (1919-1921)
Carrer del Carme, 80. Barcelona.

- Grup escolar 'Ramon Llull' (1919-1923)
Diagonal, 275. Barcelona.

- Grup escolar 'Pere Vila' (1920-1930)
Av. de Lluís Companys, 24. Barcelona.

- Escola del Mar (1921)
Now demolished.

- Grup escolar 'Collasso i Gil' (1932)
Carrer de Sant Pau, 101. Barcelona.

GRANELL, Jeroni:
- Balaguer Museum (1882)
Vilanova i La Geltrú (Garraf).

GUSTÀ, Jaume:
- Palau de la Indústria (1888)
Parc de la Ciutadella
Now demolished.

JUJOL, Josep Maria:
- Torre de la Creu (1913-1916)
Carrer de Canalías, 12. Sant Joan Despí (Baix Llobregat).

- Can Negre (1914-1930)
Torrent del Negre. Sant Joan Despí (Baix Llobregat).

- Casa Bofarull (1914-1931)
Els Pallaresos (Tarragonès).

- Church (1918-1923)
Vistabella (Tarragona).

- Torre San Salvador (1909-1910)
Passeig de la Nostra Senyora del Coll, 79. Barcelona.

- Casa Planells (1923-1924)
Av. Diagonal, 332. Barcelona.

- Casa Serra (1927)
Carrer de Jacint Verdaguer, 25. Sant Joan Despí (Baix Llobregat).

- Casa Jujol (1932)
Carrer de Jacint Verdaguer, 27. Sant Joan Despí (Baix Llobregat).

LACASA, Luis:
- Pavilion for the Republican Government at the Paris Exhibition (1937)
(in collaboration with Sert, J.L.)
Now demolished.

LLORET, Joaquim:
- Clínica Barraquer (1936-1939)
Carrer de Muntaner, 314. Barcelona.

MARTINEZ, Pelai:
- Palau de les Arts Gràfiques (1929)
(in collaboration with Duran Reynals, R.)
Passeig de la Santa Madrona. Montjuïc. Barcelona.
Now demolished.

MARTORELL, Jeroni:
- Sabadell Savings Bank (1905-1915)
Carrer de la Verge de Gràcia, 17. Sabadell (Vallès Occidental).

MARTORELL, Joan:
- Church of Les Saleses (1885)
Passeig de Sant Joan, 88. Barcelona.

MASÓ, Rafael:
- Mas el Soler (1907-1910)
Carretera d'Anglès. Sant Hilari de Sacalm (Selva).

- Farinera Teixidor (1910-1911)
Carretera de Santa Eugènia, 42, Girona.

- Casa Masó (1911-1912)
Carrer de les Ballesteries, 29. Girona.

- Casa Masramon (1913-1914)
Carrer Vayreda, 6. Olot (Garrotxa).

- Casa Cendra (1913-1915)
Carretera de Girona. Anglès (Selva).

- Casa Teixidor (1918-1922)
Carretera de Santa Eugènia, 19. Girona.

- Casa Gispert (1921-1923)
Av. Jaume I, 66. Girona.

- S'Agaró (1929-1935)
S'Agaró (Baix Empordà).

MESTRES FOSSAS, Jaume:
- Artistes Reunits Pavilion (1929)
Montjuïc.
Now demolished.

- Editorial Seix i Barral (1930-1931)
Now demolished.

- Blanquerna school (1930-1933)
Via Augusta, 140. Barcelona.
Now Institute Menéndez i Pelayo.

MIES VAN DER ROHE, Ludwig:
- German Pavilion (1929)
Parc de Montjuïc.

MUNCUNILL, Lluís:
- Aymerich i Amat Factory (1907)
Rambla d'Egara. Terrassa (Vallès Occidental).

- Masia Freixa (1907)
Carrer Volta. Terrassa (Vallès Occidental).
Now Escola de Música.

NOGUÉS, Xavier:
- The Spanish Village (1927-1929)
(in collaboration with Folguera, F., Reventós, F. and Utrillo, M.)
Av. del Marqués de Comillas. Montjuïc. Barcelona.

PERICAS, Josep M.:
- Església del Carme (1910-1914)
Carrer del Bisbe Laguarda/Sant Antoni Abat. Barcelona.

- Casa Comella (1912)
Now demolished.

- Monument a Verdaguer (1913-1924)
Av. Diagonal/Passeig de Sant Joan. Barcelona.

PUIG I GAIRALT, Antoni:
- Myrurgia cosmetics factory (1928-1930)
Carrer de Mallorca, 351. Barcelona.

PUIG I CADAFALCH, Josep;
- Casa Martí (Els Quatre Gats) (1895-1896)
Carrer de Montsió, 3 bis. Barcelona.

- Casa Puig (1897-1900)
Plaça de Vendre. Argentona (Maresme).

- Casa Garí (1898)
El Clos. Argentona (Maresme).

- Casa Amatller (1898-1900)
Passeig de Gràcia, 41. Barcelona.

- Casa Macaya (1901)
Passeig de Sant Joan, 114. Barcelona

- Casa Muntada (1901)
Av. del Doctor Andreu, 48. Barcelona.

- Casa Terrades (Casa de les Punxes) (1903-1905)
Av. Diagonal, 416-420. Barcelona.

- Casa Trinxet (1904)
Now demolished.

- Casa Quadras (1904)
Av. Diagonal, 373
Now Musical Instruments Museum.

- Casa Sastre (1905)
Carrer d'Eduard Conde, 44. Barcelona.

- Casarramona factory (1911)
Carrer de Mèxic, 36-44. Barcelona.

- Palau Alfons XIII (1923)
Plaça del Marquès de Foronda. Montjuïc. Barcelona.

REVENTÓS, Ramon:
- The Spanish Village (1927-1929)
(in collaboration with Folguera, F., Utrillo, M. and Nogués, X.)
Av. del Marqués de Comillas. Montjuïc. Barcelona.

- Flats (1928)
Carrer de Lleida, 9-11. Barcelona.

RIBAS, Josep Maria:
- Palau de l'Agricultura (1929)
(in collaboration with Mayol, M.)
Carrer de Lleida. Montjuïc. Barcelona.
Now Mercat de les Flors.

RIBES, Demetri:
- Railway Terminal (1906-1930)
Valencia.

RODRÍGUEZ, G.:
- Flats and Astoria cinema (1933-1934)
Carrer de París, 193. Barcelona.

ROGENT, Elies:
- University building (1860)
Plaça de la Universitat. Barcelona.

ROVIRA, Antoni:
- Mercat del Born (1873-1876)
(in collaboration with Fontserè, J. and Cornet, J.)
Carrer del Comerç, 29. Barcelona.

- Mercat de Sant Antoni (1876-1882)
(in collaboration with Cornet, A.)
Carrer del Comte d'Urgell, 1. Barcelona.

RUBIÓ, Joan:
- Casa Alemany (1900-1901)
Carrer del General Vives, 29. Barcelona.

- Casa Golferichs (1900-1901)
Gran Via, 491. Barcelona.

SAGNIER, Enric:
- Palau de Justícia (1887-1908)
(in collaboration with Domènech i Estapà, J.)
Av. de Lluís Companys, 16. Barcelona.

SERT, Josep Lluís:
- Flats (1930)
Carrer de Rosselló, 36. Barcelona.

- Flats (1930-1931)
(in collaboration with Yllescas, S.)
Carrer de Muntaner, 342. Barcelona.

- Joieria Roca (1934)
Passeig de Gràcia 18. Barcelona.

- Dispensari Central Antituberculós (1934-1938)
(in collaboration with Torres, J. and Subirana, J.)
Carrer de Torres Amat/Pg. de Sant Bernat, 10. Barcelona.

- Two week-end houses (1935)
(in collaboration with Torres, J.)
Garraf (Garraf).

- Pavilion for the Republican
Government at the Paris exhibition (1937)
(in collaboration with Lacasa, L.)
Now demolished.

SOLER, A.:
- Casa Heribert Pons (1907-1909)
Rambla de Catalunya, 19-21. Barcelona.

SUBIRANA, J.:
- Dispensari Central Antituberculós (1934-1938)
(in collaboration with Sert, J.L. and Torres, J.)
Carrer de Torres Amat/Pg. de Sant Bernat, 10. Barcelona.

TORRES, J.:
- Dispensari Central Antituberculós (1934-1938)
(in collaboration with Sert, J.L. and Subirana, J.)
Carrer de Torres Amat/Pg. de Sant Bernat, 10. Barcelona.

- Two week-end houses (1935)
(in collaboration with Sert, J.L.)
Garraf (Garraf).

UTRILLO, M.:
- The Spanish Village (1927-1929)
(in collaboration with Folguera, F., Reventós, R. and Nogués, X.)
Av. del Marqués de Comillas. Montjuïc. Barcelona.

VILASECA, Josep:
- Tallers Vidal (1879-1884)
Carrer de Diputació/carrer de Bailèn. Barcelona.

- Studio for three brothers Masriera (1882)
Carrer de Bailèn, 70 - 72. Barcelona.

- Casa Bruno Cuadros (1885)
Rambla de Sant Josep al Pla de la Boqueria. Barcelona.

- Batlló tomb (1885)
Via de Santa Eulàlia. Cementiri del Sudoest. Barcelona.

- Casa Pla (1885-1886)
Carrer de Pelai/carrer de Balmes. Barcelona.

- Arc de Triomf (1888)
Passeig de Lluís Companys. Barcelona.

- Casa Pia Batlló de Bach (1891-1896)
Gran Via/Rambla de Catalunya. Barcelona.

- Casa Enric Batlló i Batlló (1892-1896)
Passeig de Gràcia/carrer de Mallorca. Barcelona.

- Casa Àngel Batlló (1893-1896)
Carrer de Mallorca, 253-257. Barcelona.

- Casa Joaquim Cabot (1901-1905)
Carrer de Llúria, 8-10, 12-14. Barcelona.

YLLESCAS, Sixt:
- Casa Vilaró (Casa de la Barca) (1929)
Av. del Coll del Portell, 43. Barcelona.

- Flats (1930-1931)
(in collaboration with Sert, J.L.)
Carrer de Muntaner, 342. Barcelona.

- Flats (1934)
Carrer de Pàdua, 96. Barcelona.

SELECT BIBLIOGRAPHY

«AC, Revista» / GATEPAC. 1931-1937. (Editorial Gustavo Gili. Biblioteca de Arquitectura. Barcelona, 1975.)

BASSEGODA, Bonaventura. *El arquitecto Elíes Rogent.* (Asociación de Arquitectos de Cataluña. Barcelona, 1929.)

BLETTER, Rosemarie. *El arquitecto Josep Vilaseca i Casanovas. Sus obras y dibujos.* (La Gaya Ciencia. Barcelona, 1977.)

BOHIGAS, Oriol. *Reseña y catálogo de la arquitectura Modernista.* (Editorial Lumen. Third edition, 1983.)

BOHIGAS, Oriol. *Arquitectura española de la Segunda República.* (Tusquets Editores. Barcelona, 1970.)

BOHIGAS, Oriol and others. *Lluís Domènech i Montaner.* (Edició de Lluís Carulla i Canals. Barcelona, 1973.)

BOHIGAS, Oriol. *Arquitectura i urbanisme durant la República.* (DOPESA. Barcelona, 1978.)

BOHIGAS, O. and POMÉS, L. *L'arquitectura modernista.* (Editorial Lumen. Barcelona, 1968.)

CERDÀ, Ildefons. *Teoría general de la urbanización. Reforma y ensanche de Barcelona.* (Editorial Ariel i Vicens Vives. Barcelona, 1968.)

CIRICI PELLICER, A. *El arte modernista catalán.* (Aymà. Barcelona, 1951.)

CIRICI PELLICER, A. *L'arquitectura catalana.* (Editorial Moll. Ciutat de Mallorca, 1955.)

COLLINS, George R. *Antonio Gaudí.* (Editorial Bruguera. Barcelona, 1961.)

COLLINS, George R. i BASSEGODA, J. *The Designs and Drawings of Antonio Gaudí.* (Princeton University Press. New Jersey, 1983.)

CORREDOR MATHEOS, J. and MONTANER, J. M. *Arquitectura Industrial a Catalunya —del 1732 al 1929—.* (Caixa de Barcelona. Barcelona, 1984.)

FLORES, Carlos, *Arquitectura española contemporánea.* (Editorial Aguilar. Madrid, 1961.)

FLORES, Carlos, *Gaudí, Jujol y el modernismo catalan.* (Editorial Aguilar. Madrid, 1982.)

FLORES, C., RÀFOLS, J., JUJOL, J. M., TARRAGÓ, S. *La arquitectura de J. M. Jujol* (La Gaya Ciencia Barcelona, 1974.)

FONTBONA, Francesc. *La crisi del modernisme artístic.* (Curial Edicions Catalanes. Barcelona, 1975.)

FONTBONA, Francesc. *Del Neoclassicisme a la Restauració 1808-1888.* (Edicions 62. Barcelona, 1983.)

FREIXA, Jaume. *Josep Lluís Sert.* (Editorial Gustavo Gili. Barcelona, 1979.)

HERNÁNDEZ CROS, J. E., MORA, G., POUPLANA, S. *Guía Arquitectura de Barcelona.* (La Gaya Ciencia. Barcelona, 1973.)

JARDÍ, Enric. *Puig i Cadafalch.* (Editorial Ariel. Barcelona, 1975.)

LE CORBUSIER. *Gaudí.* (Ediciones Polígrafa. Barcelona, 1967.)

MARTINELL, César. *Gaudí. His Life. His Theories. His Work.* (M.I.T. Press. Cambridge Massachusetts, 1975.)

Memòria renaixentista en l'arquitectura catalana (1920-1950). (Col·legi Oficial d'Arquitectes de Catalunya. Barcelona, 1983.)

MIRALLES, Francesc. *L'època de les avantguardes 1917-1970.* (Edicions 62. Barcelona, 1983.)

O'NEAL, William (Editor). *Antonio Gaudí and the Catalan Movement 1870-1930.* (Papers X, The American Association of Architectura Bibliographers.)

RÀFOLS, J. F. *Modernismo y modernistas.* (Ediciones Destino. Barcelona, 1949.)

RÀFOLS, J. F. *Antonio Gaudí.* (Editorial Canosa. Barcelona, 1929.)

ROCA, Francesc. *El Pla Macià.* (Edicions La Magrana. Barcelona, 1977.)

RUBIÓ i TUDURÍ, N. M. *El jardín meridional.* (Editorial Salvat. Barcelona, 1934.)

SERT, J. Ll., and SWEENEY, J. J. *Antoni Gaudí.* (Ediciones Infinito. Buenos Aires, 1961.)

SOLÀ-MORALES, Ignasi de. *Gaudí.* (Ediciones Polígrafa. Barcelona, 1983.)

SOLÀ-MORALES, Ignasi de. *Joan Rubió i Bellver y la fortuna del gaudinismo.* (Editorial La Gaya Ciencia. Barcelona, 1975.)

SOLÀ-MORALES, Ignasi de. *Eclecticismo y vanguardia. El caso de la arquitectura moderna en Catalunya.* (Editorial Gustavo Gili. Barcelona, 1980.)

SOLÀ-MORALES, Ignasi de. *L'Exposició Internacional de Barcelona.* (Fira de Barcelona. Barcelona, 1985.)

TARRÚS, Joan. *Rafael Masó.* (Publicacions del Col·legi Oficial d'Arquitectes de Catalunya i Balears. Barcelona, 1971.)